Published by Eastern Heroes Publishing
Produced by Rick Baker

Designer
Tim Hollingsworth
Instagram: 79_design

Cover Artwork
Darren Wheeling

Printing: Ingramspark

Contributors:

UK
Rick Baker
Simon Pritchard
Paul Bramhall

USA
Robert Jefferson
Brian bankston
Jason McNeil

All rights reserved. No part of this publication may be reproduced or transmitted in any or by any means, graphic, electronic or mechanical, including photocopying, recording, taping or any information storage and retrieval system, without prior written permission of the publisher.
© 2023 Eastern Heroes.

EDITORIAL

Dear readers,

Welcome and Happy New Year! As the first edition of the year makes its way to your hands, we can't help but feel the excitement of kicking off 2024 with a bang. Although this issue should have graced your shelves in 2023, we believe it serves as the perfect way to set the tone for the year ahead.

This issue is a special one, putting the spotlight on the legendary Shaw Brothers stable. We're thrilled to bring you an exclusive interview with none other than Lu Feng, a member of the iconic "Venoms Troupe" who portrayed "The Centipede." Special thanks to Robert Jefferson and Simon Pritchard for conducting this insightful interview.

Brian Bankston contributes a fascinating article titled "CHANG CHEH'S POISONS: THE TUMULTUOUS HISTORY OF THE VENOMS," offering a deep dive into the captivating legacy of the Venoms. Additionally, Alan Donkin explores the enchanting world of Shaw Brothers posters and their remarkable artwork.

In this issue, "City on Fire" Paul Bramhall presents a compelling feature on the action movie star Wu Jing, providing readers with a closer look at his impressive career.

As always, your continued support is the lifeblood of our magazine, and we sincerely appreciate it. Without you, there would be no magazine, and for that, we are truly grateful.

Looking ahead, our next issue promises to delve into the world of directors, featuring an exclusive interview with Isaac Florentine. Renowned for his contributions to the martial arts and action genre with films like Undisputed II: Last Man Standing, Undisputed III: Redemption, Ninja, Ninja: Shadow of a Tear, and Close Range, Florentine has also played a pivotal role in launching the career of British actor Scott Adkins.

Thank you for being part of our journey, and we can't wait to share more exciting content with you in the coming months.

Keep the faith

Rick Baker

CONTENTS

2. The Rise of Shaw Studios
6. Lu Feng Interview By Simon Pritchard & Robert Jefferson
14. Ode to Gallery - With Alan Donkin
39. Chang Cheh's Poisons
50. Billy Jack - The Woodstock of Martial Arts Movies
58. Wu Jing - Hong Kong Hopeful to Mainland Hero
68. CineAsia - Interview with Cedric Behrel
72. Five Fingers of Discs

The Rise of SHAW BROTHERS STUDIOS
From Humble Beginnings to Cinematic Dominance

In the realm of cinematic history, the saga of Shaw Brothers Studios unfolds as a tale of four visionary brothers who not only broke down barriers but also shaped the trajectory of martial arts cinema. With a blend of business acumen, creative genius, and an unwavering commitment to entertainment, the Shaw Brothers embarked on a journey that would redefine an entire genre.

Entrepreneurial Roots and the Birth of Tianyi Film Company:

The narrative commences with the eldest brother, Runje Shaw, whose entrepreneurial spirit laid the foundation for what would become Shaw Brothers Studios. Graduating with a law degree at the tender age of 18, Runje diversified into textiles and other ventures before venturing into the world of Chinese opera. The pivotal moment came when he managed the Xiao Wutai theatre, setting the stage for collaboration with key figures like Zhang Shichuan, Zheng Zhengqiu, and Zhou Jianyun. Inspired by their success with "An Orphan Rescues Grandfather" (1923), Runje founded the Tianyi Film Company in 1925, joined by his brothers Runde, Runme, and Run Run Shaw.

The Golden Years and Survival amidst Turmoil:

For a quarter of a century, Shaw Brothers Studios flourished, becoming synonymous with Wuxia films that blended romance and action. During the pre-World War II era, the studio strategically avoided political statements, focusing on entertainment. However, the ban on martial arts movies by the Chinese government posed a formidable challenge. Undeterred, the brothers relocated to Shanghai, successfully navigating the constraints until the impending Japanese invasion prompted a move to Hong Kong. The war, marked by studio destruction and personal challenges, tested the resilience of the Shaw Brothers.

Post-War Triumph and Global Expansion:

In the post-war era, with Runje's retirement, Run Run Shaw took the reins of Tianyi Film Company. Exploiting a gap in the market, created by a Chinese government ban on their films overseas, the Shaw Brothers capitalized on their Hong Kong and Shanghai locations. British rule in Hong Kong and the part of Shanghai under international law shielded them, enabling global distribution. The studio's pivot to period dramas and the burgeoning popularity of Wuxia and Kung Fu genres solidified their standing as a cinematic force.

The Shaw Brothers Legacy: Iconic Films and Talent Development:

With an output exceeding a thousand films, the Shaw Brothers crafted a legacy that transcended time and borders. The strategic signing, of talent to contracts, akin to Hollywood's golden era, nurtured directors

like Chang Cheh and Lau Kar-leung, ensuring a continuous stream of masterpieces. Actors such as Jimmy Wang Yu, Gordon Liu, Cheng Pei-pei, and Shih Szu cut their teeth within the Shaw Brothers system, contributing to the studio's unparalleled success.

The Zenith and The End of an Era:

The zenith of Shaw Brothers Studios coincided with their dominance of the Kung Fu world, producing classics like "Come Drink With Me," "Flying Guillotine," "Five Deadly Venoms," "The 36th Chamber Of Shaolin," and "Legendary Weapons Of China." Yet, by 1985, faced with competition and piracy challenges, Run Run Shaw decided to close the film production arm, marking the end of a cinematic era.

The Legacy Lives On:

As the brothers, Runde and Runme, passed away in the '70s and '80s, and Run Run Shaw in 2014 at the age of 106, the legacy of Shaw Brothers Studios endures. Their 60-year dominance of the industry remains unparalleled, leaving an indelible mark on the world of Kung Fu movies. The Shaw Brothers are not just a part of cinematic history; they are the very essence of Kung Fu cinema, a legacy that transcends imitation and stands as a testament to their unparalleled contributions to the art of filmmaking.

THE LETHAL FORCE
BEHIND THE SHAW BROTHERS LEGACY

Interview with Lu Feng
By Simon Pritchard & Robert Jefferson

Lu Feng is one of the most famous actors and martial artists to come out of the Shaw Brothers studio and Kawloon, Hong Kong. We have the pleasure of working with Robert Jefferson, R4FILMS, to share his experiences with Lu Feng and asking the questions only a friend would know.

You started martial arts at the age of eight at the Junior Lu Guang Drama school. How did you end up being enrolled at the school?

I entered Luguang Opera School (Chinese opera school) when I was 8 years old because I had to test a lot of items in the entrance examination, such as body softness, bright voice, and boldness, these are all necessary conditions when studying. And I was admitted because of my loud voice and my soft body because I was young. In addition to learning singing, I also learned somersaults and weapons such as knives, guns, sticks, and sticks.

What was the school like and in which aspects did you flourish?

Our school has to perform on the stage and we must learn both literature and martial arts so that we can be competent in performances. At that time, I could sing in literary opera and fight in martial arts, so I was an all-around actor.

What made you want to get into stunt work?

Do you know? When young men reach the age of 15 and 16, they switch from a child's voice to an adult's voice, but some people can maintain the original good voice when they were young, but unfortunately, I didn't maintain the huge voice when I was a child, but fortunately, my martial arts was still very good, so after the age of 16 I performed martial arts on stage. But in that era, fewer and fewer people came to watch Beijing opera or Chinese opera, and there was less space for us to become. At that time, martial arts movies were on the rise, so the martial arts performances we learned in Peking Opera School were just right. It can be used in movies, so the movie career of martial arts actors and doubles began.

How did you meet Chang Cheh and what was it like when he wanted you to be an actor with Shaw Brothers?

Director Chang Cheh came to Taiwan from Hong Kong Shaw Brothers (SB) to shoot movies. I was lucky enough to know Director Chang Cheh because he was a martial arts actor and stand-in in films such as Marco Polo, the Fifth Patriarch of Shaolin, and Badaolouzi directed by Chang Cheh. And he finished filming in Taiwan. Afterwards, I and these brothers and sisters were brought back to Hong Kong to join Shaw Brothers (SB).

We did not become actors at the same time. Guo Zhui was already an actor in Taiwan, and Jiang Sheng and I became actors after we arrived in Hong Kong. Sun Jian also came later than us. Luo Mang and Wei Bai are from Hong Kong, and I only met them after I went to Hong Kong.

At the age of 20 you started acting in the films and for the first couple of years you played supporting roles. What lessons have you learned that have helped you in your career, if any?

Starting from a supporting role, I learned and understood the difference from previous stage performances. Stage performances will be more exaggerated and have big movements, while film performances are closer to life, and with the understanding and use of the camera, the martial arts methods are also quite different. Stage martial arts are good-looking, while movie martial arts need to be real, and the changes must be maintained. Beauty.

In 1978 you had your first leading role in The Five Deadly Venoms. What was it like filming at the time and what was your usual routine on set?

When I was filming Five Venoms in 1978, Director Chang Cheh asked me and Jiang Sheng to be his assistant director, and he also asked me to be his assistant martial arts instructor. We shoot from about 11 am to 11 pm every day.

Before shooting a certain scene, Jiang Sheng, Guo Zhui and I have to go to Director Zhang's house to discuss martial arts weapons, and fighting methods, and to make each martial arts look good. As for the daily shooting progress, Jiang Sheng and I have to convey Director Zhang's requirements and tell the actors how to position the camera and how to perform, because we are the assistant directors.

You were also credited as the Fight Coordinator, how did fight scenes develop into the fights we see on the screen?

Before the shooting of each film, I, Jiang Sheng, and Guo Zhui must hold a meeting with director Chang to discuss the weapons of each actor in the plot, fighting style, how to use the scene, and which character in the play dies.

Taking the Five Venoms as an example, all kinds of venoms, how to practice centipedes, how to practice scorpions, and snakes must be designed well, because there are various props to match, and at the same time, the moves are also designed and then only on the shooting scene (designed fighting movements).

The Five Deadly Venoms has had such a large cultural impact in the West. Kill Bill by Quentin Tarantino, Kung Fu Panda, Wu Tang Clan, video games and much more, how does this make you feel?

From my personal point of view, since the appearance of Bruce Lee, American movies have been greatly influenced and changed. Coupled with the diversification of weapons and fighting in Hong Kong and Taiwan movies, the martial arts moves in American movies are also diverse.

In the past, there was only a boxing style of fighting, but now no matter whether Marvel or recent John Wick are close to Chinese martial arts moves, because they are good-looking, real, and powerful, giving the audience a visual experience. And the Five Venoms are loved by countries such as Europe and the United States, and I didn't know until a long time later. In short, as you said, Chinese martial arts movies not only affect American movies but even animation and video games have been greatly affected and changed.

You continued to work with Chang Cheh and your Venom brothers Sun Chien, Phillip Kwok Chun-Fung, Wai Pak and Lo Meng. You made many films with them in the late 70's and early 80's. What were your best memories of this time?

When we were filming in Hong Kong, Guo Zhui, Jiang Sheng, Luo Mang, and Sun Jian became good friends because we had to shoot every day and got along happily. What I miss most is everyone's friendship. Myself, Jiang Sheng, and Guo Zhui went to Hong Kong from Taiwan, so Shaw Brothers provided a dormitory for us to live in, along with our wives (we both had wives at the time). We all became good friends. We would go to shoot, while the wives gathered together to chat and play Mahjong. We were

very happy to cooperate.

In 1979 you won Outstanding Supporting Actor at the 25th Asian Film Awards for Shaolin Rescuers. What was it like and how did this make you feel?

My feeling when I won the award was that I worked hard to learn opera and martial arts since I was a child. Director Chang Cheh gave me the space and opportunity to develop, and every cooperating friend such as Jiang Sheng and Guo Zhui also gave me a lot of help. I won the award and am very grateful to every friend and family who helped me. Most importantly, I would like to thank Director Chang Cheh.

What made you want to go back to Taiwan and start your own film company with Chiang Sheng, Philip Kuo Chue and Kuo Chui?

Director Chang Cheh, Guo Zhui, and Jiang Sheng will return to Taiwan to set up a company. The first reason is that the contract with Shaw Brothers was about to expire. The second is that the Director thinks that the three of us will go to Hong Kong from Taiwan to create another opportunity if we return to Taiwan. Or changes, but not bound by the contract, the space is larger.

Ruthless Tactics aka Ninja in a Deadly Trap, is now highly sought after, what do you remember from this film?

The film "Ninjutsu" was conceived by director Chang Cheh. The Chinese say "five elements" means metal, wood, water, fire, and earth, which themselves generate and restrain each other. This can also be used in martial arts, meaning that every martial art can have another kind of martial art as restraint, and the Japanese also have "five elements ninjutsu"

We invited "Kurata Yasuaki" to play the Japanese Five Elements ninja master, and he also found several Japanese actors to participate in the filming. The movie explains how the five elements of China and the five elements of Japan are mutually restrained. Guo Zhui, Jiang Sheng and I co-directed, and the martial arts instructor was also the lead actor. It is very hard work, but it is also very rewarding.

How did you come to Direct Ninja in the Deadly Trap?

When we returned to Taiwan to set up a company, we did everything by ourselves, so we had to take care of the director, martial arts instructor, and actors at the same time.

Guo Zhui and Jiang Sheng, have cooperated with me tacitly in our work for many years, it is necessary to cooperate seamlessly.

What impressed me the most was that I accidentally stabbed a hole in Jiang Sheng's mouth with a real spear when we were doing the "Tricks". He kept shooting.

Lo Meng told us once that Cheng Cheh fell into a man-made river on set, he accidentally swallowed the water & as a result suffered the rest of that day with diarrhea? Were you there? And do you have any funny set stories from those days?

What Luo Mang said is true, I was there that day, but Jiang Sheng and I were conveying Director Chang's instructions to the photographers and actors, telling the actors the scene we were going to shoot, it was Luo Mang who first discovered that Director Chang fell into the water, and immediately jumped into the water and helped Director Chang up.

Fortunately, Director Chang was fine, so we went home first, changed into clean clothes and went back to the set. We continued to shoot until the end of the day's work, but did you know that when the day's shooting was finished, Director Chang actually made an appointment with Jiang Sheng, Guo chased me to my dorm "play mahjong" Ha! ha!

Did you know that if we finished shooting ahead of time, Director Chang would invite us to "play mahjong"? I believe that Director Chang showed his softer side at this time, but he demanded 100% seriousness during filming.

You were acting during one of the golden ages of kung fu; did you pass on anything that you now regret?

So far I have no regrets, because I have been doing the job I love since I left school, and I have never left for a day. I believe that as long as I have energy, I will continue to shoot until I have no energy.

You have had an impressive career playing the bad guy, what draws you to these roles?

ha! Maybe I look like a bad guy by nature. My wife often says that I look fierce when I don't speak, so I don't know if it's because of this that Director Chang Cheh keeps asking me to play the bad guy.

What's your favourite non-Shaw Brothers project you've worked on or been a part of?

A non-Shaw Brothers movie? I think it would be Ninjutsu. In fact, there is another movie "Die Xian and Chopsticks Fairy" filmed in Taiwan because it is a comedy, the kind which I'd never acted in when I was at Shaw Brothers. In the film, I played Die Xian and Jiang Sheng played Chopsticks Fairy.

In reflection, what fond memories or regrets do you have?

My fondest memory is working with many great stars, like Fu Sheng, Ti Lung, David Jiang, Danny Lee, Qi Guanjun, Hui Yinghong, and too many great actors. I also studied with the famous director "Liu Jialiang", because he was director Zhang Cheh's martial arts instructor when I entered the film industry; I got a lot of knowledge about movies and martial arts from him. But it's a pity that I don't have the opportunity to cooperate with directors other than Zhang Cheh and more famous actors.

Do you prefer acting or directing?

Of course, I like to be an actor, and my major is martial arts, but because I am old, I no longer have the physical strength of my youth, and my martial arts movements may not be as fast and beautiful. Being a director or a martial arts instructor allows me to design more, newer, and better martial arts scenes, and allows the actors in the film to create the images I want, like martial arts movements, and achieve the effects I want with love and dedication. I think I now prefer directing.

Did your experience as an actor inform your current work directing film & TV in Taiwan? If so, how?

When I was an actor in the Shaw Brothers company, I accumulated experience in film, including expression, acting, martial arts changes and camera operations, I can move costumes, and lighting, because of these basic learning and experience. Therefore nowadays, I can move freely between martial arts instructor and director.

What is your favourite kung fu movie you were in? And a favourite one you had nothing to do with?

My favourite movies of mine are "Street Hero" and "Flag of Iron". A movie that's not about me? I have participated in every film directed by Zhang. We all know about Bruce Lee. I have watched each of his movies countless times. He is the only hero in my heart and the pride of the Chinese.

If you could be a part of any creative project what would it be?

I have fallen in love with movies since I was very young, and I joined this job by chance. It is also a career I like, so I have never thought about other careers. This is more than fifty years, regardless of whether the work is going well or not, I have not left., even for a day. And if you are referring to related movie projects, I think martial arts movies are the direction that will not change. I believe that if I have the opportunity, I will make martial arts movies or action movies that are different from anyone else's.

Do you remember the trip with R4FILMS through the mountains of Mexico? Would you trust Robert Jefferson to drive you around again?

Of course I remember, it was a journey worth remembering, thanks to James Valentino Santi who helped me arrange a beach house for me, and entertained me to eat Mexican food. You and another Robert (Samuels) you are all my good friends and I believe in you. I look forward to the day when Robert can drive me around again, take a stroll, and enjoy delicious food.

We also talked about our families; does your son really grasp the mark his dad has made on not only kung fu cinema, but film as a whole?

I think my son only knows that when I was

young, I was a well-known actor and now I am an unknown director. Did you know… The only movie of mine he's watched is "Incomplete".

How has fatherhood affected your worldview?

I'm not quite sure what worldview you're referring to, but as a father, I can only tell my children to try their best to pursue their own goals and ideals, no matter what the goal is, as long as it's correct, he likes it. Do your best to pursue it. Just like my pursuit and dedication to martial arts, movies and TV.

What does the future hold for Lu Feng?

My future is to be a good director, and I hope to make one or several great martial arts movies or TV one day. Once again, my love and dedication to movies and TV have not changed in the past fifty years.

Robert Jefferson: The Lu Feng story

Someone once said: "never meet your heroes". The part we say in our head goes something like; "they'll disappoint you every

time." The truth is, most famous people are actually pretty cool, some of them aren't, but then, isn't that just the way of the world?

It's 1982, I'm 10 years old. It's 2pm on a Saturday and I'm watching channel 29, a local Philly UHF station. Black Belt Theatre is on. I'm excited, this week is Crippled Avengers. A movie that still has one of the coldest lines in cinema history "I have no hands, like you have no eyes!" Proceeds to gouge both eyes out with a prosthetic metal hand. This line, of course, is spoken by Lu Feng.

That role, Silver Spear in The Kid With The Golden Arm, The Centipede in Five Deadly Venoms, Lin Yun Chi in Masked Avengers & so many more, had cemented Lu Feng in my mind as one of the most imposing figures in Asian cinema. Like countless others, those Saturday afternoon Fu-fests led me to seek to become, even if just a little taste of, what characters like San Te (36th Chamber of Shaolin) achieved through perseverance and hard work.

So I took martial arts. I wrestled, I boxed, and I took Tae Kwon-Do. Then I moved on to Hung Gar, first with a group of other enthusiasts, who would become my Si-Hings, and later with Sifu Cheung Shu Pui, Maurice Tunstall, Northern Mantis with Bilel Whitaker and a handful of others who helped shape my enthusiasm into something close to what I imagined.

That was the thing about those films; many of them had a very similar universal message: "work hard and you can overcome".

I later went on to study film at NYU, & have even managed to make a few. It is more through the latter path than the former, that I found myself in the position to meet idols like Sammo Hung, Chiu Chi Ling, Lo Meng, and ultimately, Lu Feng.

More acutely, through my partnership with Hong Kong luminary Bobby Samuels, ny Si-Hing, and one of a precious few African Americans to share screen time with Hong Kong action royalty & the only one from West Philadelphia, where I grew up a few years behind him. In short, without him, little, if any of this, would be possible, including this article.

What's meeting one of these people like? It's kind of like meeting Christian Bale, and he's 75-85 percent Batman. Or, in the case of meeting Lu Feng; imagine meeting Darth Vader, but he can do some of the stuff from the movie in real life. Silly as it sounds, I was legitimately afraid of Lu Feng as a kid, meeting him recalled some of that feeling. Getting to know him and his wonderful family over the course of a rather surreal week, made me love him.

He really is a very nice person. Kind & generous, humble, but passionate about the craft of filmmaking. He's a dad, he's a husband. He has a really mellow presence that belies the type heartless villains he's known for playing. So it really was quite surreal. Drifting between trying to remember how to order pancakes in Spanish & tripping on the fact that the

centipede is ordering eggs just a few feet away.

A moment, by the way, brought to you by Sifu James Santi, another of the kind & generous souls I've encountered on the most recent leg of my filmic journey.

In a nutshell, Sifu Santi is a kindred spirit, another martial artist inspired by an era of films that inspired many of us to take our own journey to become a master. Not only did he do so, but he became a healer, a teacher, a mentor, and, in so doing, had previously brought such luminaries as Lo Meng and Art Camacho abroad to Mexico to inspire his students through seminars, shared meals & excursions.

Bobby Samuels and a friend were in charge of hosting one of Lo Meng's US visits in 2016. On the tour, Santi (as we call him) had arranged a video shoot for a satellite member of the Wu Tang Clan & got Lo Meng aboard along with Martial Club and Ron Hall. We were to direct. On that first day in particular, we were walking to the Buddhist temple located in L.A.'s Chinatown which was to be our set. We took a back street and ran into James Lew, on another set, who we would ironically work with on Made in Chinatown two years later.

From L.A. we traveled to Tijuana & had adventures with Lo Meng which led us to being invited back the following year to Guadalajara with Art Camacho, and again the following year with today's subject…Lu Feng.

It is under these auspices which I found myself, on a number of occasions, driving Lu Feng, his wife, and his teenage son from place

羅江郭鹿孫韋傅狄錢龍王　　廣　　張
　　　　　　　　　　　　　五　十　　徹
莽生追峯建白聲龍豪翔力　　侯　虎　　
　　　　　　　　　　　　　TEN TIGERS OF KWANGTUNG

to place.

On one such occasion, in fact, we found ourselves on our way to Ensenada's famed wine country. On this particular trip, Sifu Santi had made available his 2003 Honda Pilot, a four door crossover (important to note), not a true off road vehicle, but close. Ensenada is about a 90 minute drive from the Tijuana city limits, and requires heading through a mountainous area. I'm a city boy primarily, east coast. Suffice it to say that, aside from a couple of trips to the Poconos, I have had precious little experience driving mountain roads, especially those without guard rails. It is also important to note that Bobby doesn't drive in Mexico, so when we roll, suffice it to say that I've got the Comm.

So, I have Bobby Samuels next to me in front, and in back I've got Lu Feng, his wife Lily, and teenage son Jay. We are rocketing up a two lane mountain pass. We are (obviously) riding up the right lane, and to that side is, well, nothing. A cavernous expanse of oblivion laid out to

Kung-Fu Poster Lo Mang

our right waiting for an errant mis-turn of the wheel to swallow us whole. We were the last of a 4 car caravan & our leader was pushing 70 mph. Bobby was concerned about losing our guide, I was concerned about the canyon, the curves, and the potential to become a projectile of death at any given moment. In my paranoia I somehow imagined being the sole, paraplegic survivor left of an accident killing not one, but two Hong Kong luminaries, frozen in place to endure the public vitriol behind such a mistake.

After what seemed like forever we reached the top. The pavement literally ended, blurring into a dirt road that was apparently under construction. At this point I could see our guide step out of his vehicle & engage in a brief conversation with one of the workers. A bit of cash exchanged hands, a barricade was moved & we were allowed to traverse down the other side of the mountain…on freshly packed dirt "roads" that slanted downward at distressing angles. If I were to guess, I'd estimate that we were going downward at at least a 30 degree angle, but perhaps it only felt that way.

To say that I was nervous is to say that Lu Feng has made "a film or two". The Honda seemed to be letting me know that she wasn't exactly made for this kind of work. Every few feet something creaked or groaned in the undercarriage, and a part of me was waiting for a "clunk" or metallic "pop" that would end the suspension and send us careening to the bottom and, if not a rocky grave, at least a one-way trip to wheelchair city. Behind me Sifu's nervous laughter, paired with the occasional "Oh wow" or "Oh my" let me know that the back seat experience was rather intense as well.

The old Honda survived, as did we all, and soon we found the dirt road giving way to a paved blacktop, like an old Warner Brothers cartoon.

We were now in a little town built on the backside of the mountain, where everyone looked to be living on a 45 degree angle in a fashion that rivals anything dreamed of by Dr. Seuss.

From there we drove on to our destination which was a vineyard & winery. This was also about when we found out that Lu Feng doesn't drink, like, at all. He is also a magnificently good sport. The winery was beautiful. The tour was interesting and enriching. The figurative and literal crowning jewel was the open air cafe & wine bar at the top of the mountain. The view was breathtaking. Delicious finger foods were enjoyed by all, my favorite being their take on spare ribs.

Witnessing sunset from a mountaintop overlooking the Pacific is easily a top ten experience. Add spending the day with a childhood hero..? Top five? It was awesome, and something I still think about and smile some five years later.

Footnote, and why I say Lu Feng is perhaps the greatest of sports: Sifu, in the spirit of "when in Rome…", tried a sip or two of Mexican wine. We later found out that it didn't agree with him and made him a bit ill. It's also important to note that if Lily hadn't told us, I doubt Sifu would have. Even then it was delivered as a humorous afterthought, with no malice whatsoever.

I suppose my greatest takeaway from the whole thing is the feeling that Sifu Lu Feng was approachable & kind hearted as was his family. We were there during August that year, Bobby's birthday is the 11th, Lu Feng helped throw Bobby a small birthday gathering at the seaside apartment Santi had rented for him. We ate, laughed, and smoked cigars.

He took time to talk to Santi's students, offering them little pointers during downtime. He told us stories about the Shaw days. When we saw him again in November at Demetrius Angelo's Urban Action Showcase, it was like reuniting with old friends, family even. He didn't have to do any of it and I'll always be grateful for the experience.

My best advice for anyone meeting someone famous, especially someone of whom you are a fan is: take a deep breath and be normal. These people are just people. Start with "hello" and take it from there. Try not to be nervous, and keep it appropriate. If you're meeting in a professional setting, be professional. Like any other social scenario, let things happen naturally. If you have a burning question for that person, you may or may not get the chance to ask it, and that's okay. Overall, be thankful and remember, most people will never get the opportunity you have. Most of us will only see famous people through a screen. Truly, I have been blessed.

R4FILMS LLC

Robert Jefferson is President at R4Films LLC. R4Films specialise in the action film genre. Creating digital motion pictures for all platforms and media. R4Films offer full fledged production needs from start to finish.

R4Films offer stunt coordinators, post-production facilities and in-house editors for all post-production needs. R4Films' experienced team specialises in every aspect of the process, from video production, 3D animation, photography and soundtrack music.

ODE TO GALLERY

THE FILM POSTERS OF THE VENOM MOB

BY ALAN DONKIN

I have a complicated relationship with the movie posters of the Venom Mob. When Rick asked me to take a look at them, I used my Sherlockian mind palace to find the relevant section, and… found my face making that expression you make when you walk into the toilet at your local boozer. I remember becoming consciously aware at some point a few years ago that I'm just not a fan of them. I seem to recall thinking that the artwork and designs were lousy, and not befitting such an iconic group of actors who produced a memorable body of excellent films. How could they get these posters so wrong? It was Shaw Brothers, who produced so many incredible posters in the 1960s and 1970s, promoting films featuring a fantastic group of stars. The repeated misfiring annoyed me.

Then I recalled a piece I did with Matt Routledge a while ago, where we briefly compared the Hong Kong and Thai posters for The Five Venoms (1978). And you know what? They were both decent. He and I both preferred the Thai variant, but during the conversation, I actually took the time to look at the HK variant properly. Previously, I'd dismissed it as dull, but on closer examination, I developed a new-found appreciation of it.

Armed with a fresh determination to look at the posters of the Venoms mob in a little more detail, I set about my task. It's been interesting. Some still fail to convince me that they're anything other than awful, but others have revealed a certain charm and quality that I didn't see before. Without further ado, I present a gallery of Venoms posters separated into three categories: The Champions (of which there are more than two!), The Rescuers (insofar as that they have rescued their credibility in this survey) and the Ruffians (who are most definitely not magnificent). Or, more prosaically: good, ok and poor.

THE CHAMPIONS

The Five Venoms (1978) – Thai variant
A colourful, lively, dynamic design that showcases a nice mix of fights and poses. I love the Mount Venomore arrangement. It's like two different posters – the bottom half is dark and mysterious, the top half bursting with life and energy. Such clashes shouldn't work, but this one does.

Crippled Avengers (1978) – HK and Thai variants

I've lumped these together because they're much of a muchness. There's some different font colouration in some of the words, and the Thai version has minimised the original text to the foot of its own text, but the designs are essentially the same. The blue and red backgrounds are striking, and the way the entire design seems to lean to the left is interesting. There's a nice balance of profiles and action poses. For a Venoms poster, it's a winner. Amazing film, too, which may be colouring my opinion.

Kid With the Golden Arms (1979) – HK variant

There's perhaps an overdose of orange here, some of the drawings are 'rudimentary' (I think that's the most polite way of putting it), and the English font looks stupidly out of place. I can't help but enjoy this design, though. It's full of action and energy. Little touches like the leaping silhouette on the left side make it appealing. It feels like a throwback to earlier Shaws designs.

Legend of the Fox (1980) – HK and Thai variants
Talking of early Shaw designs – these are class. The HK one especially, with its blocky 3D text and moody lighting. The pockets of fighting taking place on top of the title is a masterclass of design, and the faces of the Venoms staring out from the blood red clouds is very evocative. Excellent.

Kid With the Golden Arms (1979) – Thai variant

Like the HK version, I wouldn't say that the drawings of the stars are particularly great, but there's a real sense of quality in this design. The background colours are far more varied than the HK design, but they blend together beautifully. I like the arrangement of the figures, facing the direction that they're emerging from. They're action poses, too, not just faces. They're lifted from the original arrangement, but presented differently. The huge weapon on the left side of the image is a great touch – it draws your eyes without dominating. The cherry on the cake is that the little leaping figure has made it to this variant! Stupid, I know, but I like the way the artist decided to produce something very different to the home territory design, while retaining some key features.

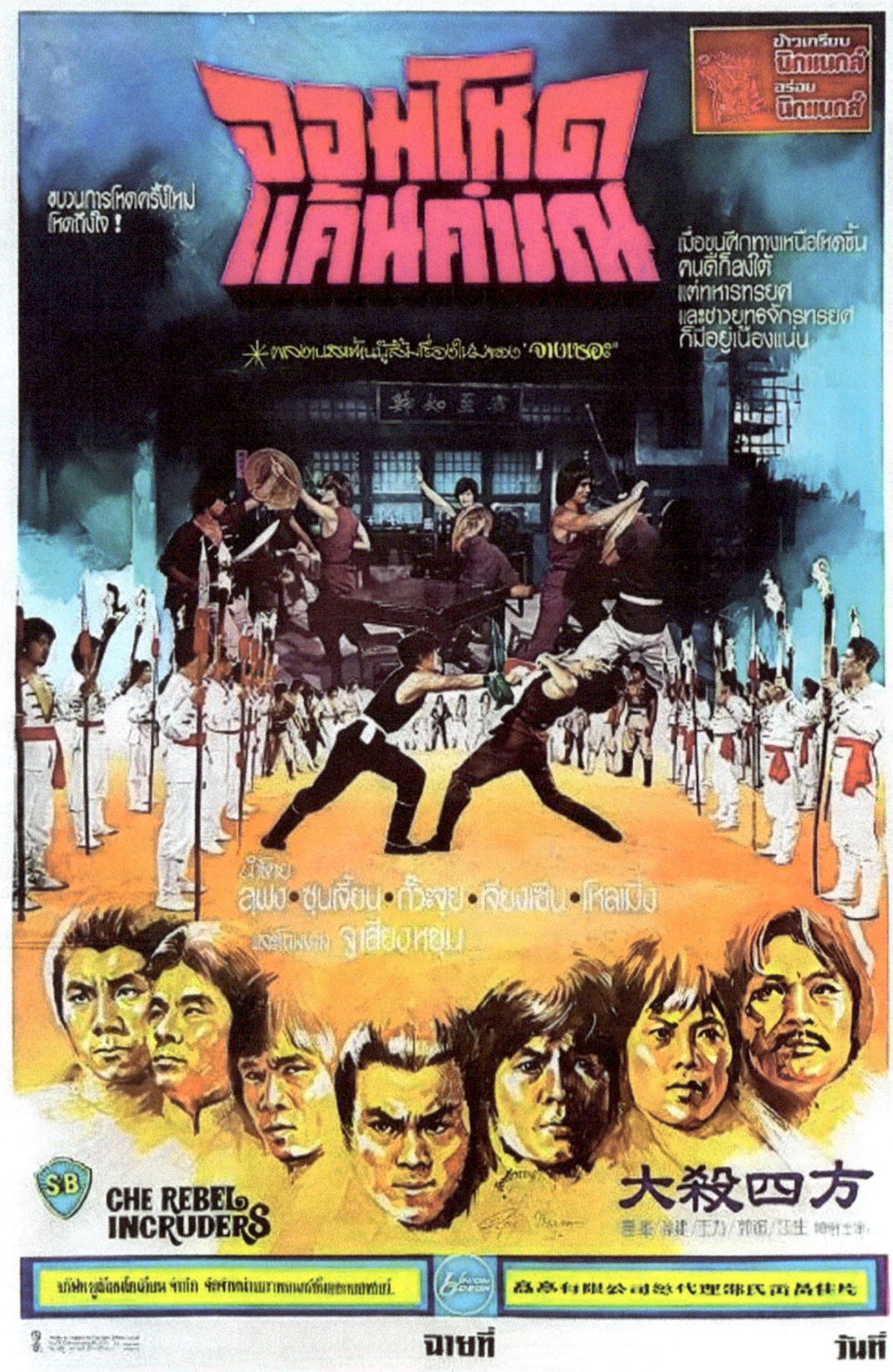

The Rebel Intruders (1980) – Thai variant
This is a high-quality design, and superior in every way to the HK version, which hasn't made the cut in this section. The blue and black background at the top is wonderful, and contrasts very effectively with the yellow and orange in the bottom half. There's a great mix of photos and drawings here. The image chosen in the centre acts as both a visual barrier between the two halves, and a way to draw the viewer into the design – it's like stepping into the combat arena. The Venoms are drawn skilfully, grabbing your attention without overwhelming the poster. Everything about this poster is great. Even the pink font works.

Ten Tigers of Kwangtung (1980) – HK variant

There seems to be two versions of this poster. They are very similar apart from some text arrangements and the main title font. I prefer the one without the English name – I love the way the title is echoed. This is a relatively simple design that works because of that very fact. The ten silhouettes atop the mountain, sun bursting behind them, representing virtue and righteousness, with their portraits illuminated by the beams. It's a great effort.

Heaven and Hell (1980) – HK variant
Rounding off this section is this rather splendid effort. I'm not actually too enamoured towards the main photo. It's the background colours and details I really like. The title is stunning – it's pure early 70s Shaw epicness. The yellows, oranges, greens and blues are a potent combination, creating a montage that's a real feast for the eyes.

THE RESCUERS

Life Gamble (1979) – HK variant
Someone loves their shades of pink. It's certainly a striking poster, I'm just not wholly convinced for the right reasons. The composition of the design is fine – the concentric circles are the focus, with the English title sitting on it at the top. The faces are nicely done, all facing the same way, and there's some wider action shots at the bottom. The black border at the foot of the page is a welcome distraction from the pink. It's just too pink.

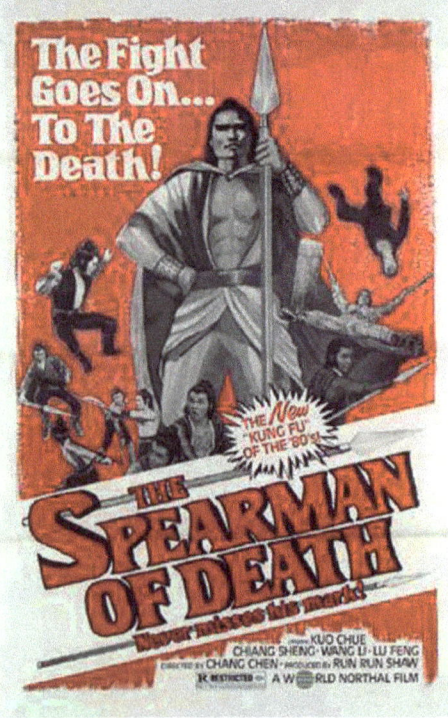

The Flag of Iron (1980) – HK, French and US variants
Oh joy. More pink. To be fair to the HK version, it's not overkill, but it's a colour that contributes to the overall unremarkableness of the design. I like the faces in the flag, but that's about it. Everything else is mediocre, at best. The French design packs more of a visual punch, with some dazzling colour choices, but I wouldn't call it a great poster. The US variant lacks that visual spark, but I quite like the 'one coat of blood' paint job in the background, with its untidy bordering. On the whole, a trio of posters that fail to ignite much in terms of excitement or artistic appreciation.

24

The Rebel Intruders (1980) – HK variant
I would say that this poster is at the higher end of this category. It's a sophisticated design, with the Venoms separating the action scene from the title. The colour choices match well, and the overall arrangement is pleasing. Compared to the Thai variant, though, it's weak. The bottom quarter of the poster is bland, and the brown lettering doesn't do the overall effect any favours. I appreciate that many will disagree, but for me, it's a little bit of a missed opportunity.

Invincible Shaolin (1978) – HK, Thai and US variants

They're ok. Nothing more, nothing less. The HK original is probably the best of the trio. The background is balanced better than the Thai version, and benefits from the darker lower third. The designs are fine, but do they sell the film? I wouldn't say so. They're a lazy pair of designs. At least the US one tries to be different, with adventurous colour choices and a bold, blocky font.

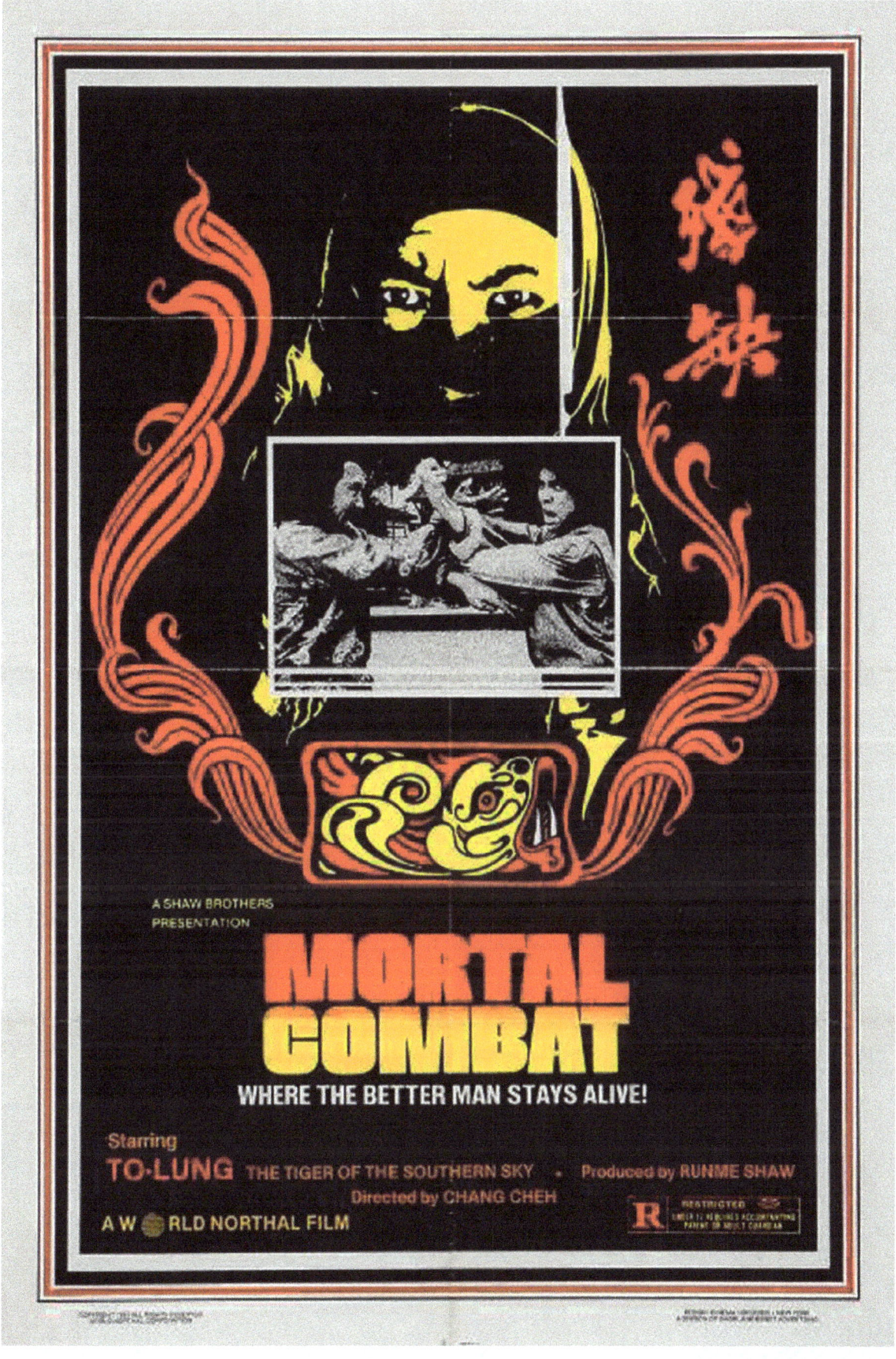

Crippled Avengers (1978) – US variant
I acquired this poster years ago as part of a batch. My initial reaction was unfavourable, but I've come to consider it a decent poster. The colour choices have a big impact on this turnaround. The red, orange and yellow shades really work against the starkness of the black background, and the single framed image in the centre provides a nice counterpoint to the cartoony nature of the rest of the design.

Masked Avengers (1981) – HK variant

The best part of this poster is the green and yellow text at the top, with the thick black outline. The worst part is the English text. I mean, what is that meant to be? The blue is out of place and partially obscured, and the way it's been plastered on at a random angle reminds me of a stamped packing crate. It's absolutely rotten. The rest of the design is average, with a combination of sketches and photographs. There's more to see than you initially presume, but it's just not a standout effort.

The Five Venoms (1978) – HK variant
One I've come to appreciate more and more. It's still not top level, but there's far more subtlety to the design than I originally credited. The gradation of colours in the text is lovely, and the way the character 'shadows' grow from the actors at the top is really effective. There's some neat colour work in them, too. The black and white faces and background tone reveal the dark nature of the film, but the players being illuminated at the top suggest that heroism is the order of the day. So close to being a great poster.

The Sword Stained with Royal Blood (1981) – HK variant

Cards on the table. It's an extraordinary design. The top half of the poster is dark and busy, the bottom half a riot of colour. The text is beautiful and gorgeously outlined. The composition is skilled and striking. I'm just not sure that the main drawing that dominates the entire poster is my cup of tea. I may be horribly wrong here, but it reminds me of the art deco movement – all ostentatious curves and 'look at me' colours. It's all down to personal taste. I appreciate the ingenuity, I'm just not sold on the execution.

Two Champions of Shaolin (1980) – HK variant
There are two great things about this poster. The first is the shadows of the weapons. The second is the 3D title text, with its white, grey and black shading, and yellow outlining. It's a superb piece of design. The rest of the poster is completely and utterly tedious. Who on Earth can look at this and feel anything other than ambivalence? A wasted opportunity.

Shaolin Daredevils (1979) – HK variant
This effort faces the opposite problem. There's too much going on. It's like someone has tipped the contents of a kaleidoscope onto the page. It's a shame, because individual components are skilled and effective. The title text is echoed with different colours. There's plenty of action. There's little locket-style portraits. Unfortunately, put together, it's just a mess. There's an overload of rustic colours, too.

House of Traps (1982) – HK variant

Another to file under 'pfft'. There's some good work on show. The traps bordering the Venoms is a strong design choice, but the colour selections are just … dull. Shaw Brothers seemingly didn't know how to present English text effectively, as this is another example of it being poorly presented. A shame – with a few tweaks, this could have been a stunner.

Ten Tigers of Kwangtung (1980) – Thai variant

This was incredibly close to being a champion poster, but I can't ignore the iffy renditions of two of the characters. They remind me of some of the art seen on Ghanian posters in the 1980s. They're too cartoony. It's a pity, because the colours and arrangement on the rest of the poster are very competent indeed. It's a busy poster, but one that doesn't feel swamped, due to the careful positioning of various elements, and bold colour choices.

THE RUFFIANS

Shaolin Rescuers (1979) – HK, German and US variants
The HK version is the best, but it's such a poor poster. Text seems to take up sixty percentage of the poster, and not in an epic way. The English text is a tagged on afterthought relegated to the bottom corner. The only part of the poster I like is the ripped red effect under the title. The other two variants are horrendous, lacking in style and creativity in a way that makes me want to vomit with frustration. It speaks volumes that I find a lobby card more visually appealing than these three. At least it has some half-decent bordering to separate the elements.

Magnificent Ruffians (1979) – HK variant
I'll probably upset a few people with this one. The black is effective. The blood splatter is good. I like the scroll. I like the shadows of the actors. It should work. But I really don't like this. I can't even articulate why. Perhaps it's the utter lack of any meaningful context. It's like the designer has said: here's the title, here's the actors. And left it at that. Where's the life? The excitement? The dynamism? It's just utterly nondescript and suggests nothing about the film itself. In the process of typing this, I feel like I've maybe been harsh and should promote it, but at the same time, I do find the poster a crushing disappointment.

Ode to Gallantry (1982) – HK variant
This isn't a bad poster. It just makes me want to avoid the film like the plague. Phillip Kwok's expression is a massive put-off, and it reminds me of those wacky posters that I really struggle with. There's some nice shading work here and there, but as a design to entice me, it fails miserably. The blue plastered along the bottom is a clumsy choice, and the English text is lousy. Again!

Kid With the Golden Arm (1979) and Two Champions of Shaolin (1980) – US variants
Here we are, folks. The bottom of the barrel. I couldn't even be bothered to give these two posters separate write-ups. They're terrible. Lazy, uninspiring rubbish. And yellow … so much yellow. Yeah, I really dislike these.

Summary

I am always aware in these opinion pieces that people will be shaking their heads and calling me all kinds of (probably true) dismissive expletives. After all, art is a matter of personal taste. I do wonder whether or not many will agree with me: that the Venoms have suffered from some pretty uninspiring poster designs over the years, with examples that don't always reflect the stature of their films and performances. Like I said at the beginning, I've ended up liking more than I thought, and my appreciation for certain entries has grown. But, on the whole, I still find their poster oeuvre depressingly underwhelming.

Many thanks to Toby Russell and Phil Jablon for the use of their images.

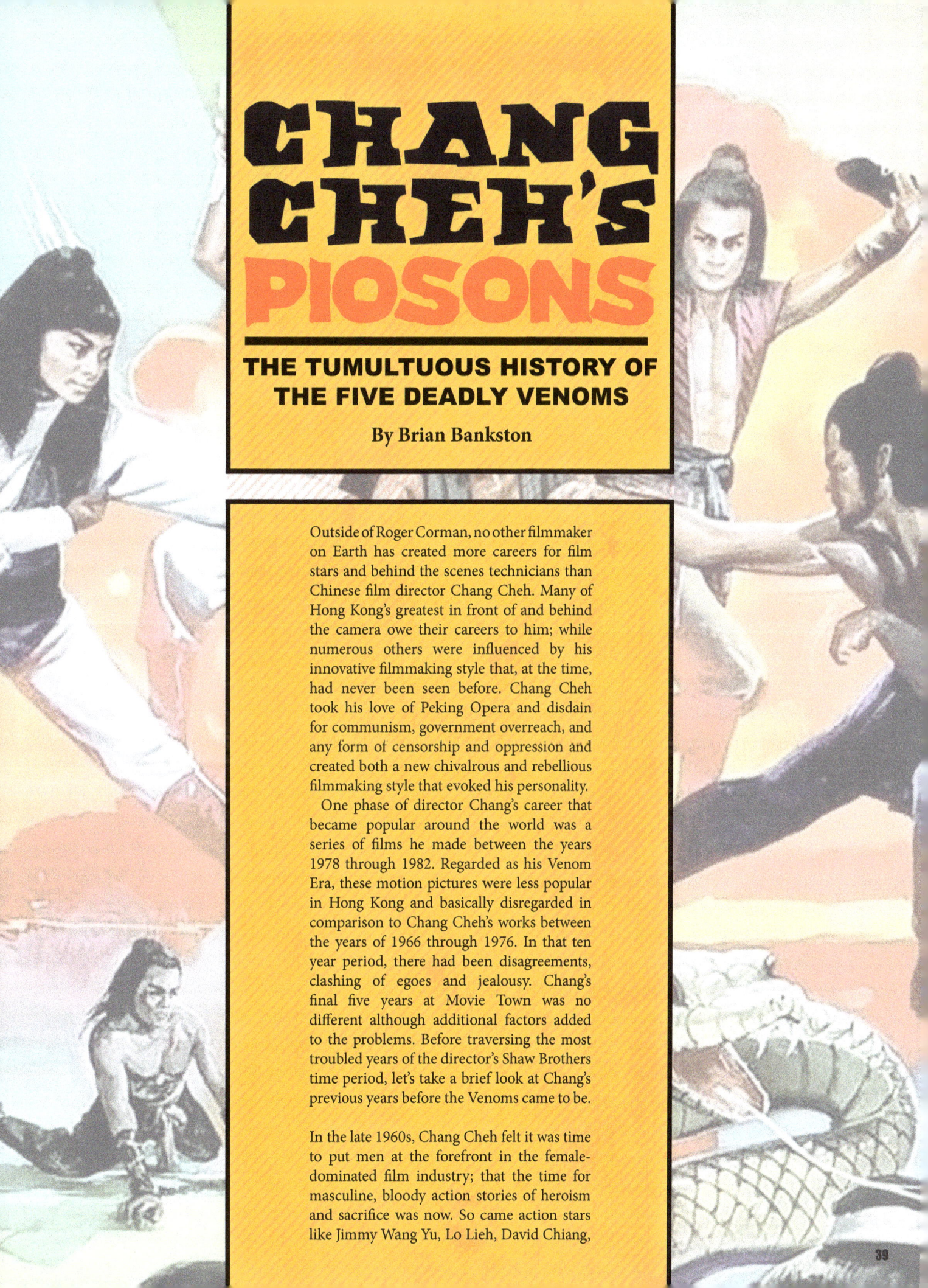

CHANG CHEH'S PIOSONS

THE TUMULTUOUS HISTORY OF THE FIVE DEADLY VENOMS

By Brian Bankston

Outside of Roger Corman, no other filmmaker on Earth has created more careers for film stars and behind the scenes technicians than Chinese film director Chang Cheh. Many of Hong Kong's greatest in front of and behind the camera owe their careers to him; while numerous others were influenced by his innovative filmmaking style that, at the time, had never been seen before. Chang Cheh took his love of Peking Opera and disdain for communism, government overreach, and any form of censorship and oppression and created both a new chivalrous and rebellious filmmaking style that evoked his personality.

One phase of director Chang's career that became popular around the world was a series of films he made between the years 1978 through 1982. Regarded as his Venom Era, these motion pictures were less popular in Hong Kong and basically disregarded in comparison to Chang Cheh's works between the years of 1966 through 1976. In that ten year period, there had been disagreements, clashing of egos and jealousy. Chang's final five years at Movie Town was no different although additional factors added to the problems. Before traversing the most troubled years of the director's Shaw Brothers time period, let's take a brief look at Chang's previous years before the Venoms came to be.

In the late 1960s, Chang Cheh felt it was time to put men at the forefront in the female-dominated film industry; that the time for masculine, bloody action stories of heroism and sacrifice was now. So came action stars like Jimmy Wang Yu, Lo Lieh, David Chiang,

Ti Lung, Chen Kuan Tai and Alexander Fu Sheng. The first film to exemplify this was his 1967 swordplay picture THE ONE-ARMED SWORDSMAN. Its surprise HK$1.5 take at the box office meant more manly movies were on the march to silver screens across the various Asian territories, and Chang Cheh was leading the charge.

Something else Chang Cheh was fascinated by was the spectacle and even beauty in righteous heroes dying for chivalrous causes, breathing their last amid a whirlwind of blood and gore. Chang was so good at depicting the hero's death that virtually every other director got on the bloody bandwagon to outdo each other in spectacular death scenes.

Spurting plasma was all the rage till Hong Kong's Film Censorship Office cracked down on big screen violence in 1973. There was an uptick in crime on the streets of HK and Chang Cheh's on-screen brutalism was being blamed for it. Films were withheld from release due to violent content or depictions of institutions deemed controversial. Chang Cheh got around this by using red tints and converting overly gory action from color to B/W. In some cases like ALL MEN ARE BROTHERS (completed in 1973 but not released till 1975), subduing the color wasn't enough and whole chunks of footage needed to be removed.

Director Chang had jumpstarted so many careers, his growing stable of film stars were broken up into classes. The First Generation class was Wang Yu, Lo Lieh, and Cheng Lieh. Not every member of each class were breakout stars (like Cheng Lieh), but were given pushes in an effort to connect with audiences. Generation #2 was the deadly duo of David Chiang and Ti Lung; who were then joined by Chen Kuan Tai in 1972. Wang Chung belonged to this group too. The Third Generation brought moviegoers the likes of Alexander Fu Sheng, Chi Kuan Chun, Gordon Liu, Wang Lung Wei, Liang Chia Jen, Li Chen Piao, Jaime Luk Kim Ming, etc. But it was Chang Cheh's Fourth Generation of film stars that brought him his greatest international recognition. The irony is that this class were not as popular in Hong Kong as they were in Occidental parts of the world. This article details the short history of Chang Cheh's internationally beloved group of actors. They're not held in the same regard on the domestic front as their big brothers like Ti Lung and Chen Kuan Tai; but outside Hong Kong, their remarkable staying power has gotten stronger over the years.

In prior groups, director Chang would have a few actors who gained fame while a few others had less levels of success. Then

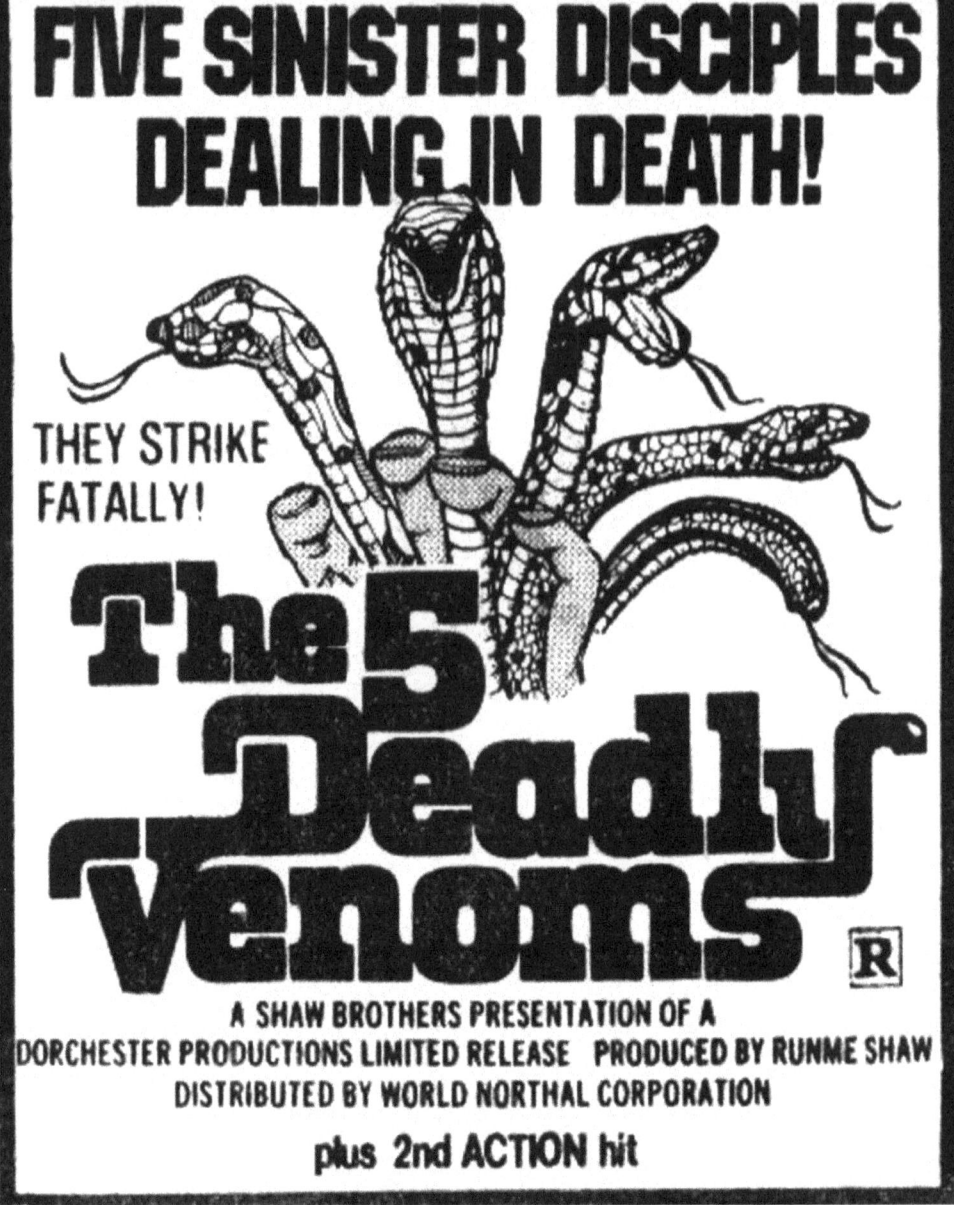

there were those who would always turn up as background or minor supporting players. With his Fourth class, the director intended to promote six actors equally in the hopes of making the entire group popular with audiences. This new faction would become well known around the world as "The Five Venoms", or the "Venom Mob". The first film to officially introduce them was the seminal hit, THE FIVE VENOMS (1978). These six new faces were Kuo Chui, Lo Mang, Sun Chien, Wei Pai, Lu Feng and Chiang Sheng. Lo Mang and Wei Pai were from Hong Kong while the other four were from Taiwan.

Three of these men were the main driving force behind the Fourth class, those being Kuo Chui, Lu Feng and Chiang Sheng. They returned with the director from Taiwan after Chang closed down his quasi-independent company, Long Bow, or Chang's Film Company. Ironically, had Chang Cheh not moved his operations back to Shaw Brothers, there likely would never have been a FIVE VENOMS at all. Director Chang had intended to remain in Taiwan much longer than the two years he was there. Shaw's capital was funding his enterprise, but eventually, Chang Cheh wanted to be his own boss and signed a deal with the Jin Hua Film Company to deliver a set amount of movies that they would distribute in Taiwan while Shaw Brothers would distribute in Hong Kong.

The deal Chang signed with Jin Hua Films stipulated he complete eight films a year for them. He also had to have SEVEN MAN ARMY done in time for Chinese New Year in Taiwan. When the contractual stipulations were not being met, the two sides renegotiated terms, but problems continued--leading to a dispute over Taiwanese distribution of *THE NEW SHAOLIN BOXERS*. Jin Hua's three bosses then filed fraud charges against Chang Cheh in October of 1976 for HK$1,000,000 plus interest. In the end, all sides settled out

of court. Run Run Shaw paid Jin Hua nearly HK$1,000,000 in the settlement. Planned Long Bow productions were canceled and *SHAOLIN TEMPLE,* already promoted as a Long Bow picture, was moved to Hong Kong to resume filming there. Chang's disastrous comedic Kung Fu flick, *THE MAGNIFICENT WANDERERS (1977),* was the last completed Long Bow production before it closed its doors. And off to Hong Kong went two dozen or so Taiwanese stuntmen and soon-to-be actors... including Kuo Chui, Lu Feng and Chiang Sheng.

Upon his return to Shaw's, Chang Cheh signed a new contract for five films a year and a salary of HK$1,000,000 a year. Meanwhile, the two dozen Taiwanese stuntmen director Chang brought back to Hong Kong with him weren't welcomed by everyone at the studio. Director Liu Chia Liang (Lau Kar Leung) had a major falling out with director Chang in Taiwan in June of 1975 and this rivalry carried over into the Shaw Brothers Studio. Some of the Taiwan guys would venture out to watch filming going on in the many factories. This annoyed Liu Chia Liang leading him to place

signs around basically stating "No Taiwanese allowed". The situation became uncomfortable till actor and martial artist Shan Mao, acting as mediator, met with the elder Liu over drinks and discussed things. Afterward, there were no more problems. Sadly, Shan Mao would be murdered in March of 1977 after the drunk actor had a violent dispute with a taxi driver.

By early 1977, Chang Cheh had made plans to gradually introduce new faces in movies like THE CHINATOWN KID and LIFE GAMBLE. Originally, there were four potential new stars—those being Sun Chien, Kuo Chui, Li Yi Min, and Lo Mang. Sun Chien was getting a hefty role in CHINATOWN KID (1977) while the other three were being showcased in major roles in Chang's LIFE GAMBLE that was filmed in 1977, but not released in Hong Kong till 1979. The film hit Taiwan theaters before Hong Kong in 1978. The reason for the delay was Chang Cheh had decided to introduce his new stars in a film tailored exclusively for them; and LIFE GAMBLE wasn't the motion picture to do that. Elsewhere, all four were starring in the newly reshot version of HEAVEN AND HELL, which began its second voyage to the screen in 1977 but didn't arrive till 1980.

Li Yi Min had worked as an actor for Chang Cheh at Long Bow in Taiwan, co-starring in pictures like SEVEN MAN ARMY (1976) and MAGNIFICENT WANDERERS (1977). He would leave for Hong Kong to complete SHAOLIN TEMPLE (1977) and to also appear in THE BRAVE ARCHER (1977). Li Yi Min didn't stick around in Hong Kong for very long, though. He returned to Taiwan to make films there; and in one instance, acted in a behind the scenes capacity on THE SEVEN COMMANDMENTS OF KUNG FU (1979).

Many Taiwanese performers Chang Cheh recruited and brought to Hong Kong on the numerous occasions he went there either felt alone in the then British colony or they felt they didn't fit in. One issue was a language gap. Many didn't speak Cantonese so they would congregate with those who were comfortable in communicating in Mandarin. This would be an issue of sorts within the Venom group once they were officially christened in 1978.

With Li Yi Min gone, Chang introduced his new Fourth Class members to the media—consisting of six new faces; those being the aforementioned Kuo Chui, Lo Mang, Lu Feng, Chiang Sheng, Sun Chien, and Wei Pai. Chang Cheh's plan for the six newcomers was to make them all stars—showcasing them in the films they were assigned to. As it were, a number of issues would arise that prevented this from going according to the plan. These issues involved more than just disgruntled film stars.

The martial arts choreographers consisted of Leung Ting, Robert Tai Chi Hsien, and Lu Feng. Both Tai and Lu Feng were Taiwanese while Leung was born in Hong Kong. A closed-door student to Bruce Lee's famous Wing Chun teacher Yip Man, Leung founded his own system as Wing Tsun. He was known around the world and was a popular teacher in Hong Kong. However, he was far less so when he became a martial arts choreographer for Chang Cheh's group made up primarily of Taiwanese stuntmen.

Leung Ting worked under Chang Cheh on six of his films. The most famous of these is THE FIVE VENOMS (1978). The others include THE BRAVE ARCHER PART 2 (1978), LIFE GAMBLE (1979), the original version of TEN TIGERS OF KWANG TUNG (1980), the reshot version of HEAVEN AND HELL (1980), and his last being INVINCIBLE SHAOLIN (1978). Reportedly, he didn't get along with Kuo Chui, Lo Mang and apparently anyone else. This is possibly why the martial arts scenes in THE FIVE VENOMS (1978) are less impressive compared to the story built around them.

The last straw was when director Chang took

issue with the way Leung was choreographing Wei Pai's Wing Chun style in INVINCIBLE SHAOLIN. With problems persisting, Chang Cheh had enough and decided Leung Ting had to go. Chang contemplated bringing back Lee Ka Ting, a little-known action instructor from Chang's THE CHINATOWN KID, NAVAL COMMANDOS and THE BRAVE ARCHER (all 1977).

Chang wasn't excited about bringing Lee back either, citing in an interview in 1978 that he was lazy but if he had the choice between the two, he'd take "a lazy person before the one that makes trouble. It's one thing to affect a single individual, and another when you affect the entire class".

By 1979, Robert Tai would leave and embark on a solo career; so with just Lu Feng remaining as an actor and choreographer, Kuo Chui and Chiang Sheng would join him, creating the famous Kung Fu trifecta of Chang Cheh's Fourth Generation. Unfortunately, the problems within the group would continue, complicating what would ultimately be a short run at the box office before Jackie Chan changed the industry overnight.

When the six actors who were being formally introduced in THE FIVE VENOMS (1978) joined Movie Town, they were offered contracts ranging from 3-8 years, or no contract at all. Wei Pai was the only actor of the six to choose the no-contract option. He did four films in the Venom series—one of which was left unfinished due partly to Wei leaving the studio. That picture, TEN TIGERS OF KWANG TUNG, was among the titles that had to shut down due to Alexander Fu Sheng's injuries in 1978 and 1979. Reshoots for TEN TIGERS began approximately two years after shooting started. Wei Pai would then begin work on an independent Kung Fu movie tentatively titled 'Master Tian' co-starring alongside Charles Heung, Li Hai Sheng, and Tommy Lee, aka Gam Ming. When Wei left that production, the film was rewritten and all footage with him reshot. Now bearing the title of GOOSE BOXER, the new film had new actors added. Tommy Lee was no longer in the cast, and instead was the film's martial arts choreographer. With a bad reputation for abandoning film productions, Wei Pai managed to find a home at Golden Harvest where his career went nowhere. He starred in John Woo's high-profile LAST HURRAH FOR CHIVALRY (1979), the title character in THE CHEEKY CHAP (1980) and Golden Harvest's 100th film THE YOUNG MASTER (1980) directed by Jackie Chan to name a few. Despite his presence in major

films that signaled the death of the traditional Kung Fu feature and the birth of a new, modernized style, Wei Pai's career dissipated into obscurity.

With Wei Pai gone, Chang Cheh remained adamant about maintaining six leading actors. For films like CRIPPLED AVENGERS (1978) and SHAOLIN RESCUERS (1979), he filled the gap with bigger names like Chen Kuan Tai on the former and Jason Pai Piao on the latter. Both men were former stuntmen and martial arts instructors turned actors. Chen of course was made famous in Chang's BOXER FROM SHANTUNG (1972). Pai tried to attain stardom at the independent company Yang Tze Films but it eluded him till he moved to television and became a household name playing Guo Jing on the LEGEND OF THE CONDOR HEROES TV series from 1975.

Both of these films were highpoints in Chang Cheh's career, and of special note during this period of his Shaw Studio days. SHAOLIN RESCUERS is made even more special in that Lu Feng won the 'Most Outstanding Supporting Actor' award at the 25th Asian Film Festival in 1979. Winning the award took the frequent movie villain by surprise, allowing him some time in the spotlight all to himself. He would even sing on stage at the ceremony, backed by Gordon Liu on guitar. Sadly, momentum for Chang's Fourth Class would gradually diminish from here. And there was still the matter of bringing in a new member of the group.

Director Chang would find his sixth actor to complete his Iron Hexagon; that man being Wang Li, a Taiwanese martial arts instructor. Like many others, Wang had previously worked under the direction of Chang Cheh at Long Bow, but declined to join the director in Hong Kong at that time. When he arrived in late 1978, he was formally introduced in a stand-out fight sequence in SHAOLIN RESCUERS (1979). Wang would receive lead villain status in 1979s THE DAREDEVILS, possibly the most intricately plotted of the Kung Fu films the Venoms made; although it never really comes to life till the amazing finale. This was also the first film where the local box office began dipping below the HK$1 million mark.

THE REBEL INTRUDERS (1980) was an intriguing premise that once again allowed for all members of the Venoms to shine on-camera. It was an important film, but for the wrong reasons. This was the production where tensions began between members of the Venoms and the lineup's eventual dispersion. A rift developed between Kuo Chui and Lu Feng. Reportedly, Kuo stopped performing anything designed by Lu Feng. Allegedly, there were rumors hinting at jealousy due to director Chang using more of Lu's ideas than Kuo's. There was more to this brief feud that, according to Chang Cheh, would take up to six hours to explain it all. To fix the problem, both men were left off the cast list for one film and only allowed to perform behind the camera. So Kuo Chui didn't appear in TWO CHAMPIONS OF SHAOLIN (1980) and Lu Feng was left off the casting for ODE TO GALLANTRY (1982).

Additionally, neither man would receive a pay increase. Money was a recurring issue with Kuo Chui. He would receive increases and seemingly be satisfied with them, only to later voice his displeasure that it wasn't enough.

Meanwhile, Lo Mang was repeatedly voicing his irritation with his having to die all the time. This reached its zenith during the filming of THE DAREDEVILS (1979). Lo became agitated over his character dying early into the picture and demanded the script be changed. Director Chang explained to him his role and exit from the movie was important to the script as well as a major highlight and would not be altered. Lo also wanted more leading roles, particularly more in which he survived. One thing Lo did like about his part in THE DAREDEVILS was his costumes. He loved the three sets of clothes so much he requested to keep them after filming wrapped. However, the studio didn't allow the actors to keep the costumes made for their roles. Director Chang saw how much this meant to the vocal young actor and made arrangements to purchase the clothes for him. Both star and director reportedly had no more heated issues afterward.

Something else that seemed to potentially cause some ripples within the group was communication. At this stage in the lineup, Lo Mang was the only one who didn't speak Mandarin; so he didn't mingle with the others very much. Sun Chien, the kicker of the Venoms, seldom interacted with the group, even though he was Taiwanese. He had a dog and kept a small farm on top of the dormitory he lived in. Aside from his girlfriend, he kept mostly to himself. Lu Feng was quiet with reporters till he became comfortable with them; while Chiang Sheng was the same spirited fellow off-screen as he was on it.

In December of 1979, the Five Venoms split up. Sun Chien was the first of them to go down the proverbial mountain. In later interviews he was asked about working with his co-stars under director Chang and Sun's reply was somewhat vague. He gave the impression he never felt like he was part of the group, stating he had always kept distance between himself and others; citing further-- "People should be treated equally to maintain good relations". Reporters at the time pointed out he was much happier with his post-Venom career,

even though the parts were smaller.

Lo Mang was next to go. He'd been repeatedly vocal about wanting more leading roles; but was nonetheless taken by surprise when, in January of 1980, Chang Cheh told him he was letting him go to work for other directors. After Chang gave him the lead in TWO CHAMPIONS OF SHAOLIN (1980), Lo wanted more like it. He had hoped to get the part of Hu Fei in LEGEND OF THE FOX (1980). That movie was already shooting before the part had been cast. Lung Tien Sheng, a Taiwanese actor who had already been a lead or supporting player in a dozen or more Kung Fu pictures, was also up for the role. Then there was Chen Hsiao Hao...

Also in late 1979, Chang had went to Taiwan to recruit more talent. Reshoots for the halted TEN TIGERS OF KWANG TUNG would soon begin and the new men Chang brought back were an integral part to what would ultimately be one of the director's weakest motion pictures.

There were six new performers total. The aforementioned Lung Tien Sheng was the most experienced as he'd already been in the Taiwanese film industry for nearly a decade, but was an unknown commodity in Hong Kong. Chen Chi Sheng and Su Wei Chen were also from Taiwan. The former was a Peking Opera acrobat and the latter was a Taekwondo instructor who hoped to become a film star. Three others were picked from Shaw's Training Academy. Chen Shu Chi looked like a shorter version of Lo Mang, while Chen Han Guang had the most innocent of faces. Both of these men played Lu Feng's monkey fighters (along with Chen Chi Sheng) in TWO CHAMPIONS OF SHAOLIN, and the mace-wielding Chong Brothers in LEGEND OF THE FOX (1980).

Finally, there was Chen Hsiao Hao (or Chin Siu Ho), the youngest of the new five making up the ill-fated Fifth Generation. They were quickly disbanded largely by the actors themselves. As mentioned earlier, most of them felt out of place in Hong Kong and desired to return to Taiwan. Their prospects in the film industry weren't good so that was a factor. That five of them all had "Chen" in their names compounded things. Of this group, only Chen Hsiao Hao went on to fame. He wasn't a superstar in the vein of David Chiang or Ti Lung, but was a popular actor. The Shaw company would see a bright future for him, so it was they who plucked Chen from Chang's camp and rewrote his contract.

As for Lung Tien Sheng, he said in an interview in 1981 he felt more like a tourist

in Hong Kong than an actor. He was up for the lead in LEGEND OF THE FOX, but after he reportedly told Chang Cheh he didn't understand the role, the director basically called him a "country boy" and Chen Hsiao Hao got the part. Lung was originally up for the role Chen got in TWO CHAMPIONS OF SHAOLIN as well. He did make a magnificent impression in Chang's THE FLAG OF IRON (1980); and in an important and strong supporting role in THE SWORD STAINED WITH ROYAL BLOOD (1981).

By this point, it was becoming clear to Chang Cheh his plan to create six stars together wasn't going to happen. Jackie Chan's SNAKE IN THE EAGLE'S SHADOW, and especially DRUNKEN MASTER (both 1978), had redefined the Kung Fu genre by injecting dollops of humor. Chan's bumpkin and Yuen Siu Tien's beggar Kung Fu master characters seemed to hook the audience almost by accident. DRUNKEN MASTER was the #2 hit of the year with HK$6.7 million. THE FIVE VENOMS was Chang's biggest hit of his official Venom movies, coming in at #14 for the year and HK$1.8 million.

With the wild success of Chan's two shoestring indy productions, other producers saw big dollar signs and some 20 Kung Fu comedies went into production at the same time in 1978. These were largely cheaply made pictures with little to no plot, but audiences had tired of the serious martial arts production. The type of bloody heroics pioneered by Chang Cheh had fallen out of favor with the majority of Hong Kong patrons. By 1982, the industry would drastically change—taking on a new modernized style that made the Shaw's period-set adventures look antiquated in comparison.

FIVE ELEMENT NINJAS (1982) was intended to have been Chang Cheh's last movie on his contract with Shaw Brothers. Lo Mang was brought back and he was excited to be working for his master again. Lung Tien Sheng had a strong supporting role as well. Chao Kuo, a promising newcomer, seemed to be a potential rising Kung Fu star. Ricky Cheng Tien Chi and Chu Ko visually exploded on the scene with some astonishing martial arts choreography, but audiences were moving away from what was deemed old-fashioned filmmaking.

Before FIVE ELEMENT NINJAS went into production, Chang's remaining Fourth Class returned to Taiwan to try working independently. Chang Cheh went with them carrying his 5EN script that would be reworked into NINJA IN THE DEADLY TRAP (1981). This type of "returning a favor" occurred while Chang Cheh was still in Taiwan struggling to keep Long Bow afloat. With a deadline to meet and a lawsuit to avoid, Chang's protege Wu Ma came to help him get films like SHAOLIN AVENGERS (1976) completed without delays. Chang Cheh had written another Shaolin script that Wu Ma made as SHOWDOWN AT THE COTTON MILL (1978). Chang Cheh would later do his own version as TWO CHAMPIONS OF SHAOLIN. Now, director Chang was helping his three original Venom trio get a film of their own off the ground.

Kuo Chui was directing for the first time and found the ordeal so distressing he didn't wish to discuss all the problems he encountered. He didn't want to leave Movie Town in the first place, so he returned there after his ninja adventure was finished. He wound up what filming remained for his mentor and then went to work for other directors. As for Lu Feng and Chiang Sheng, they stayed in Taiwan.

Meanwhile, Chang Cheh went back to Hong Kong and had some new faces with him, Ricky Cheng, Yao Li, and Chu Ko. Yao Li would only appear in HOUSE OF TRAPS (1982) before giving the business. Ricky Cheng and Chu Ko would help make 5EN a remarkable final film for the director's Shaw contract.

The Shaw's were apparently pleased with it and they managed to convince Chang to sign a new contract with them, only this one had unusual stipulations attached to the deal. It was for 2 years and 6 films in total. However, if either side is unhappy with the

situation, the contract will be dissolved. So Chang directed THE WEIRD MAN (1983), his official last film for Shaw Brothers on his new contract. It would seem nobody was particularly pleased with the outcome, the film bombed, and Chang Cheh left to found Chang Ho Company in Taiwan, taking Ricky Cheng with him, and reuniting with Lu Feng and Chiang Sheng.

In the end, Kuo Chui (or as he's known more prominently now as Philip Kwok) had the biggest career of the original Five Venom lineup. He not only worked locally but overseas in Europe and America, even doing action design on the Bond adventure TOMORROW NEVER DIES (1997). Lo Mang went on to have a good career in the industry and remained in the spotlight. Lu Feng went into television and gradually worked more behind the scenes, so he stayed busy. Sun Chien never became famous but stayed active till the early 1990s. Chiang Sheng, who was the most comical and jovial of the bunch, had the saddest ending. With the roles he enjoyed at Shaw Brothers nonexistent in Taiwan, and any chance at moving up from an assistant director to a director not coming, his life took a turn for the worse. Sadly, divorce and alcoholism took their toll on the vibrant acrobatic film star. He died in August of 1991.

As for director Chang Cheh, he burned through his retirement his wife set aside for him to found Chang Ho. He likely had no regrets. Chang loved filmmaking. In a 1979 interview he remarked he had three great loves in his life: money, movies and, paramount above all else, his wife.

Looking back at the Fourth Class Era, the films may have been fun and entertaining Kung Fu excursions, but from a technical standpoint, they were mostly retreads of past glories. Chang Cheh was repeatedly trying to recapture the spark of his earlier years. SHAOLIN RESCUERS (1979), for example, was a Kung Fu version of the director's 1971 Eastern Western THE ANONYMOUS HEROES. Then there was THE FLAG OF IRON (1980), which was a remake of 1971s THE DUEL, but taking place in a different time period. Director Chang was seemingly out of ideas and the limited innovations were just copies of what others were doing. Chang would then switch to adapting Jin Yong's works since director Chu Yuan made Wuxia popular again after the release of the top ten hit KILLER CLANS in 1976. Director Chang's 80th movie was heavily promoted, only it wasn't a Kung Fu spectacle starring the Venoms, but his fourth and last in his BRAVE ARCHER series, 1982s BRAVE ARCHER AND HIS MATE, starring Alexander Fu Sheng, Huang Shu Yi (Gi Gi Wong), and his re-assembled Venoms lineup.

The industry was changing. From 1978 to 1982, Chang Cheh was grappling to find a foothold in the genre he created fifteen years earlier. It was likely for the best that he didn't alter his style much because we may not have gotten such incredible comic book action pictures like THE REBEL INTRUDERS, THE MAGNIFICENT RUFFIANS (both 1979), MASKED AVENGERS (1981) and FIVE ELEMENT NINJAS (1982) from Chang's later Shaw period.

The actors that made up the Venom Mob and their revolving door of performers may not have had lasting impact in Hong Kong as a team but they certainly did everywhere else outside of it. Had they come into the industry two or three years earlier, their careers may have turned out differently. We the fans will always have these gems to enjoy over and over again; and hopefully, a new generation of fans will be able to appreciate and marvel at the various members of the Poison Clan rocking the world once more.

THE WOODSTOCK OF MARTIAL ARTS

Celebrating Peace, Love and [...] with Billy Jack! BY Jason McNeil

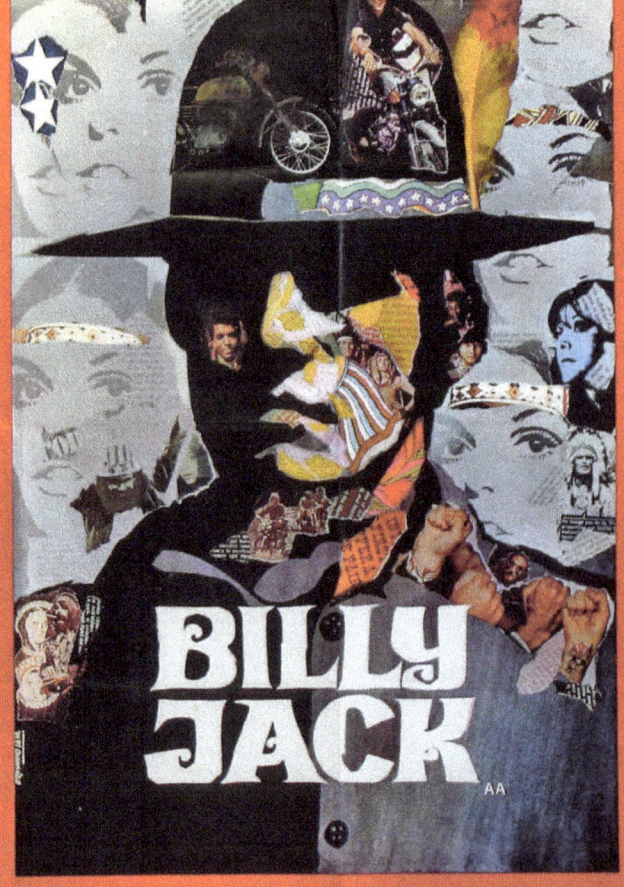

The year was 1967 and, with the exception of the Green Hornet's black-clad chauffeur (on a show no one was watching), NO ONE was kung-fu fighting! Not yet, anyway....

While British audiences were treated to Emma Peel karate chopping her way across their TV screens in a series of increasingly tight jumpsuits, across the pond in America, cinematic martial arts were still hovering somewhere between James Cagney's rolling throws and breakfalls from the World War 2 era Blood on the Sun and Bat-fans being assured that, in addition to her "photographic memory" and skills as a professional librarian, Barbara Gordon was eminently qualified to join Gotham City's war on crime because she had earned "a brown belt in judo."

By and large, Western audiences were still a few years shy of the massive explosion of 70's chop socky action, kicked off (so to speak) by Bruce Lee's triumphant, albeit posthumous, return to international big screens, David Carradine's "Kwai-Chang Caine" on the small screens and the tsunami of Bruce-sploitation and 70s kung-fu mania that would follow – as has been well documented here in the pages of Eastern Heroes.

In 1967, however, the hippies were hip, the counter-culture was going mainstream and everyone was all about social rebellion, peace, love and understanding. Also, bell-bottomed jeans, free love and weed. Lots and lots of weed. Hell, we were just 18 months from Woodstock......

Unexpectedly, into the midst of all this hippieness and lack of any mainstream martial artsiness strode Tom Laughlin, alongside his wife and movie-making partner, Delores Taylor, bringing a high-kicking, martial arts action hero the likes of which most movie-goers had never before seen, while somehow managing to balance the "peace and love" message with a barrage of on-screen ass-kickery.

Not coincidentally, they also introduced the west to the high-kicking Korean martial art of Hapkido, via Tom Laughlin's own martial skills and those of his teacher and stunt double, Master Bong-Soo Han.

The Born Losers (1967)

According to Laughlin and Taylor, they had written the original draft of their Billy Jack script in 1954, and had been unsuccessfully trying to get it made for over a decade. Laughlin flatly stated, on many occasions, that even though the main character was a veteran and there was an action element to the movie, no one "back then" wanted to make a movie about discrimination towards American Indians.

So, when the husband and wife team noticed the sudden popularity of "outlaw

TOCK
RTS MOVIES
Kicks to the Face!

biker movies" they hastily threw together a motorcycle gang flick with Billy Jack (played by Laughlin) as the hero. The story, itself, was based on a real incident in 1964 that got a lot of press, where members of the Hells Angels motorcycle gang had been arrested for raping two teenaged girls.

The movie version, titled The Born Losers (also the name of the fictional biker gang), manages to pull off the difficult task of balancing its hippie/anti-authoritarian attitude with a handful of excellent high kicking action scenes (again, courtesy of Laughlin and Master Han, doubling him.) The story goes that the bikers roll into town and start menacing the locals, and end up assaulting some of the young girls. Billy Jack steps in to defend the townspeople and teenagers, and is promptly arrested by the local police. While the bikers are fined $150 for their various and sundry crimes, Billy Jack is made to pay $1,000 for "discharging a firearm" and has to sell his Jeep to pay the fine. The motorcycle gang continues to act up, and the local authorities continue to combine incompetence and corruptness to punish the "righteous" until Billy Jack and his hippie pals have no choice but to take the law into their own hands!

Much kicking follows.!

Fun Facts: The Born Losers features an early appearance by Jeff Cooper (Circle of Iron) and a late appearance by Jane Russell! "Jane Russell had a magnificent career," said Laughlin, "but then, like so many young ingenues, her career suddenly dried up. So she wanted to show that she could still work and perform, like Shelly Winters did, and that's how she ended up in this picture."

Billy Jack (1971)

After the relative success of The Born Losers, it seemed obvious that Laughlin and Taylor would finally get their long-delayed passion project, Billy Jack, to the big screen. However, as is often the case in indie cinema, the path continued to be a long and winding road.

Hot on the heels of The Born Losers, filming began on Billy Jack in the fall of 1969, in Prescott, Arizona. However, for reasons that vary depending on who's remembering, American International Pictures pulled the plug half-way thru, and it was well over a year before 20th Century Fox picked up where AIP had left off, allowing filming to be completed. Surprisingly, 20th ultimately declined to distribute the finished film they had helped pay for, but Warner Bros. finally stepped up and agreed to do Billy Jack's distro.

Upon release, critical reviews were mixed, but something about the film hit home with movie-goers. Viewed thru the lens of hind-sight, it is perhaps easy to see how the somewhat slapdash combination of high-kicking Korean Karate violence and the film's central message of "Summer of Love" ethics and values could come off as a little ham-fisted, but it absolutely, 100% captured the zeitgeist of the time. American culture was quite famously arguing with itself and Billy Jack reflects all the different voices that were part of the cultural cacophony.

Not to mention that, hippie stuff aside, there are some absolutely awesome fight scenes in the film, a few of which have moved into the realm of the iconic. Even if you haven't seen the movie, you can probably quote the "kick to the side of your face" scene verbatim!

The film, itself, is a fairly simple story of – again – Billy Jack, the American Indian, Vietnam Veteran, martial arts expert who has appointed himself protector of the local young hippies – in this case, a school-full of them – facing off against the small town redneckery that wants to smash their hopes and dreams, limit their free thinking, force them to conform, knock up the pretty girls and ship the young men off to 'Nam to fight in an endless war for profit. Etc, etc.

The final scene, where Billy Jack surrenders to the authorities for the "crime" of protecting his young charges, is famously dialogue-free, and set entirely to Coven's song, "One Tin Soldier." It could be argued that that scene, alone, is one of the most moving cinematic moments of all time – certainly of the Flower Power Era.

Despite its mixed reviews, Billy Jack was a hit with audiences and was, for awhile, the most successful indie movie of all time! A sequel was, of course, inevitable.

Fun Fact: Billy Jack features an early appearance by a young Howard Hesseman (credited under the pseudonym "Don Sturdy") as the hippie school drama class stand-out, "Howard." This was, of course, a full seven years before young Howard burst into pop culture prime-time as Disc Jockey "Dr. Johnny Fever" on the hit TV show WKRP in Cincinnati and a full 12 years before his criminally Oscar-ignored turn as "Smooth Walker" in 1983's Doctor Detroit!

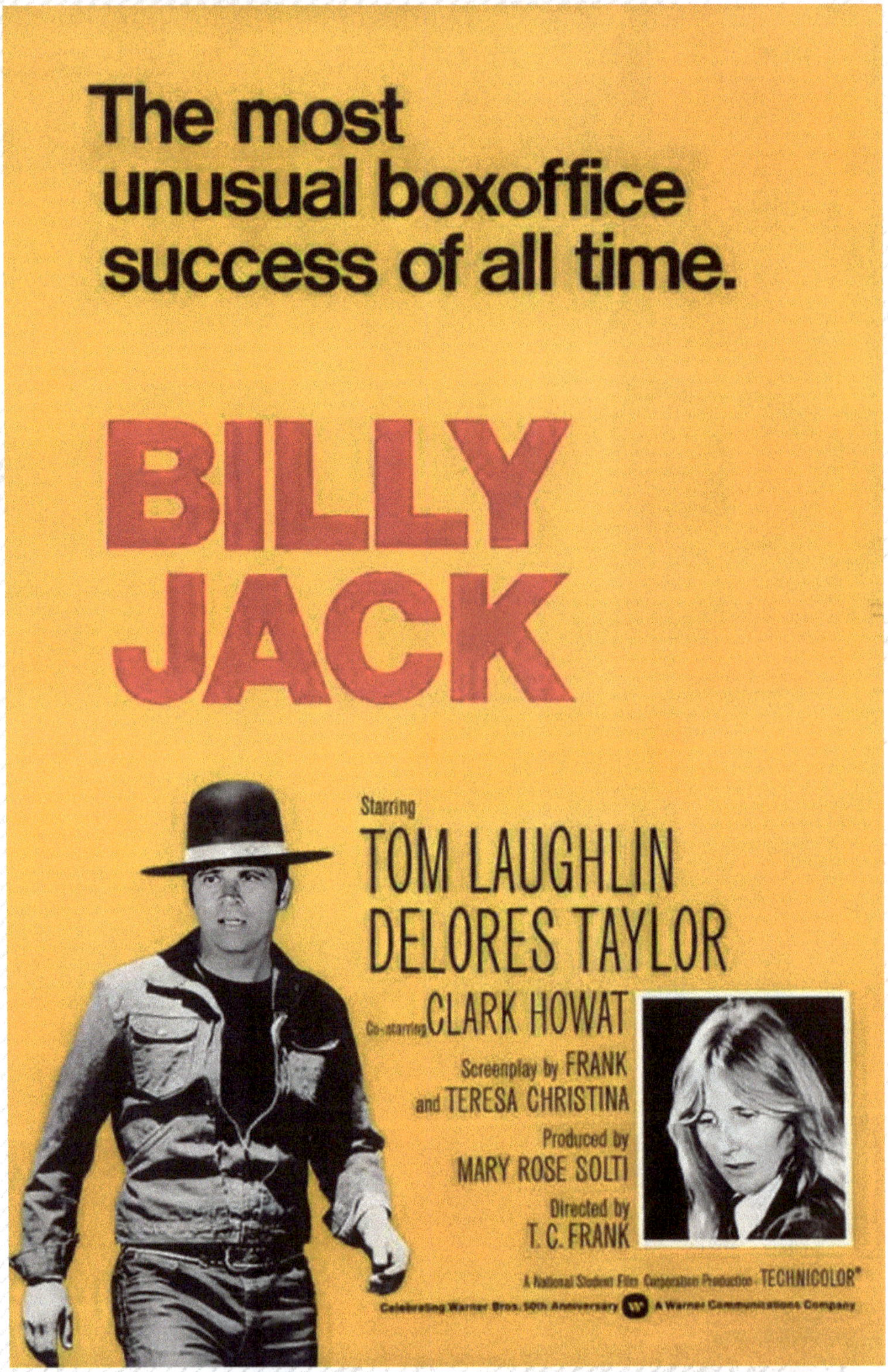

The Trial of Billy Jack (1974)

Having come off the unexpected and unprecedented triumph of making the most successful independent movie in history, Tom Laughlin and Delores Taylor, clearly flush with success and, perhaps, a bit drunk

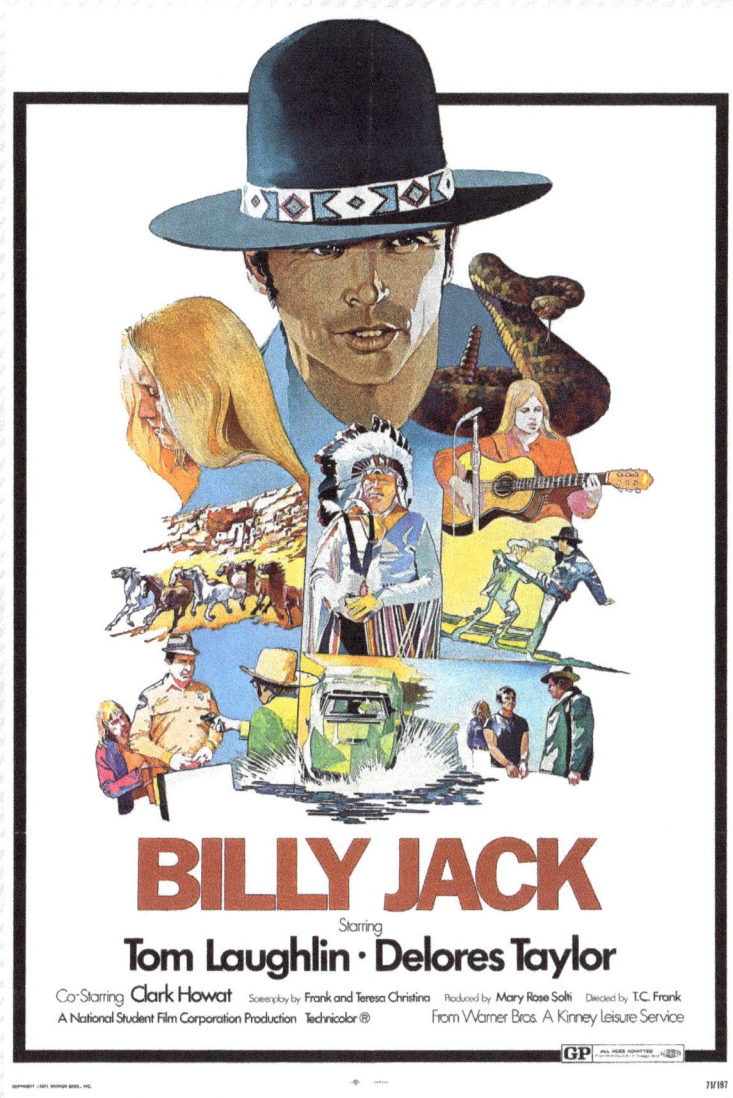

with power, turned out what we must assume they thought would be their move to the Next Level: The Trial of Billy Jack.

Ehhhh......

Let's ask Tom Laughlin what he thought of the movie, a quarter of a century later: *"If I had to do it over, I would cut a lot of this out. But there it is."* - Tom Laughlin (2000).

Clocking in at nearly three hours long (although shorter edits are floating around), The Trial of Billy Jack picks up where the last movie left off – with Billy Jack facing the inept and corrupt justice system at his trial for protecting the hippie students from the redneck townspeople in the previous film.

And, because its the early 70s, we all know that society is full of problems, and the government is corrupt, and that there are a whole host of societal ills that could be easily corrected if only the old people in positions of authority would listen to the teenagers who just want them to love one another and fix everything wrong in the world with flower power, right?

Well, if you didn't know that, don't worry, The Trial of Billy Jack will remind you of that, over and over and over, for – as mentioned before – just shy of three hours.

Having managed to pull off a Reese's Peanut Butter Cup mix of "two great tastes that taste great together" (martial arts action and hippie culture), Laughlin and Taylor clearly decided that what the audience wanted more of was great, high kicking, Hapkido action.....

Just kidding. The movie is mostly just endless, endless hippie preaching and pontificating, about everything from the government to war to child abuse to how, if we just allow children to make their own decisions and support and back them up 100%, then they will always, just naturally, do the right thing. (Clearly, someone hasn't read Lord of the Flies....)

Also, there's a whole thru-line about police brutality of protesters that is clearly a reaction to the then-recent killings at Kent State. And on and on and on.

Billy Jack doesn't even get into his first "protect the hippies" fight until an hour and 48 minutes in! (Although we do get a tiny bit of martial arts action when the students are being given a self-defense class just shy of the one hour mark.)

Hot on the heels of the first fight, the second fight scene shows up at right around the two hour click, bringing Bong-Soo Han, himself, into the fray rather than just him disguised at Billy Jack's double.

There are some interesting things in The Trial of Billy Jack, including a weird side trek where Billy Jack undergoes an Indian ritual wherein he takes some hallucinogens, rappels down into a desert cave, confronts some demons and ultimately slaps Jesus (!!!) but, all in all, the movie just comes off as preachy and bloated. No doubt based on the awesomeness of its predecessor, The Trial of Billy Jack opened at Number One in US Theatres, where it stayed for three weeks, grossing $9 million dollars in its first five days! After that, though, it sort of fell off the map and did abysmally overseas. Tom Laughlin opined at the time that the film's poor reception outside the USA was the result of an American governmental conspiracy to force the film to be "banned in almost every country in the world" to hide the

brutal social truths and "scorching exposes" from foreign audiences! When pressed on the subject, however, he admitted that he had "no supporting evidence" for his theory.....

Real Line from the Movie: "Pretty soon, we became recognized as one of the few places that could successfully help parents who battered their children!"

Billy Jack Goes to Washington (1977)

It must've seemed like a great idea on paper:

"Let's do a remake of the 1939 classic, Mr. Smith Goes to Washington, but with Billy Jack instead of Jimmy Stewart! And we'll get Frank Capra's son, Frank Capra, Jr, on as Producer! That way, we can update a classic film and talk about how corrupt Washington is....."

Nope.

Nope, nope, nope.

If you wanted all the sophomoric pontificating of the previous film, but with less action, then this is the movie for you!

The first evidence of any martial arts, anywhere in the film, comes in at the 50 minute mark, with Billy Jack karate chopping a glass top table. Then, five minutes shy of an hour in, a fight finally breaks out. That having been said, the fight in question is a pretty good one, notable for both Tom AND Delores kicking ass. (She takes her boots off and everything!)

Worth watching for completion's sake, Billy Jack Goes to Washington has one or two good things in it, but mostly just falls flat.

Fun Fact: The end credits of Billy Jack Goes to Washington include "Stunt Coordinator: Hal Needham" and the movie came out the same year as Smokey and the Bandit! Hal certainly turned out better films that year, but – hey! - as we say in the biz, "Work is work!"

Another Fun Fact: During the end credits of Billy Jack Goes to Washington, the aforementioned iconic song from the second film, "One Tin Soldier" plays, but this time, its a cover version sung by one "Teresa Laughlin." I'm gonna take a wild guess and say "Tom and Delores's kid?"

The Return of Billy Jack (1986)

In the mid-80s, Tom Laughlin and Delores Taylor decided the time was right to return to the Billy Jack Well, with a story about the Titular Hero taking on child pornographers in New York City.

Sadly, only about 15 minutes of footage was shot before an accident with a "breakaway bottle" that didn't break away injured Laughlin during a fight scene. By the time Tom recovered, the production was out of money and never resumed.

For those who care to dig, there is footage from the unfinished film floating around, showing Billy Jack, dressed as a priest, beating up some 'Mob goon' looking thugs.

Truly sad, because – c'mon! - who wouldn't want to see a Hapkido master beating up pedophiles? I know I'd watch that!

Post-Script

Sadly, Tom Laughlin passed away in 2013, and his beloved Delores Taylor followed in 2018, so the time of Billy Jack is over.

Or is it? Say what you will about the various and sundry films of the Billy Jack series, but they are definitely unique, in both martial arts entertainment and to cinema in general. They, to differing degrees, entertain, occasionally educate and provide a permanent snapshot of that time in the American hippie counter-culture. Laughlin and Taylor had their own, unique muse and a shared vision of what art and movies could do, and they more or less achieved it – writing, producing, starring and even directing (under a pseudonym) - with a startling level of success that no one – except, perhaps, they – could have predicted. We should all aspire to such artistic heights, and hope to leave such a legacy to live on after us.

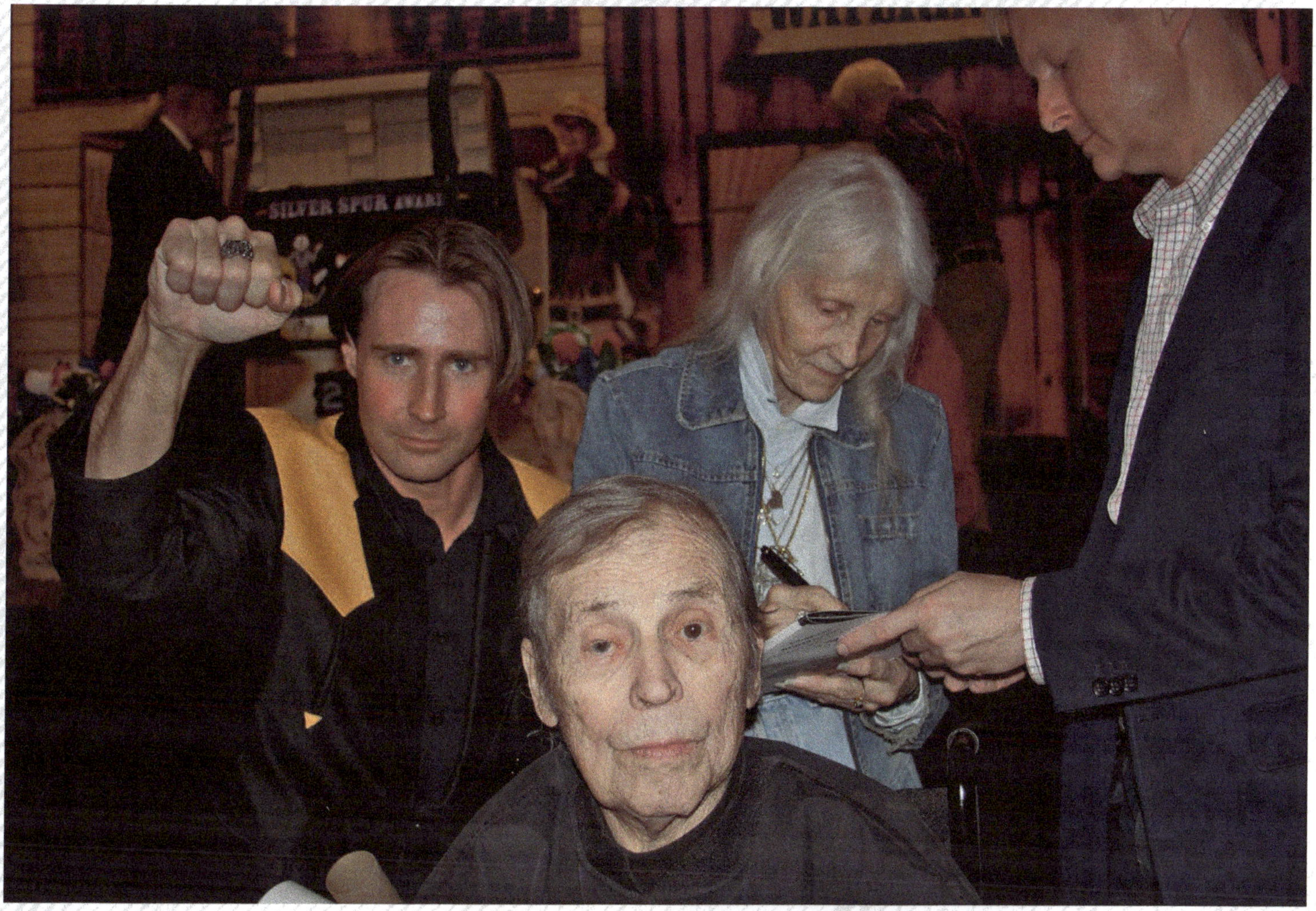

DVD BONUS FEATURES:

Yes, we're all film nerds. Yes, we watch the bonus features and listen to the commentary tracks. We're reading Eastern Heroes magazine, so that's pretty much a given.

That having been said, if you are at all interested in MAKING movies - especially low budget and indie projects – then make sure you check out the "Commentary" tracks, recorded in 2000, included with Image Entertainment;s "The Complete Billy Jack Collection" DVD Boxed Set! Its almost as if Tom and Delores knew that young filmmakers would be the main folks digging into their bonus features, and the tracks are a non-stop description of how they saved money,

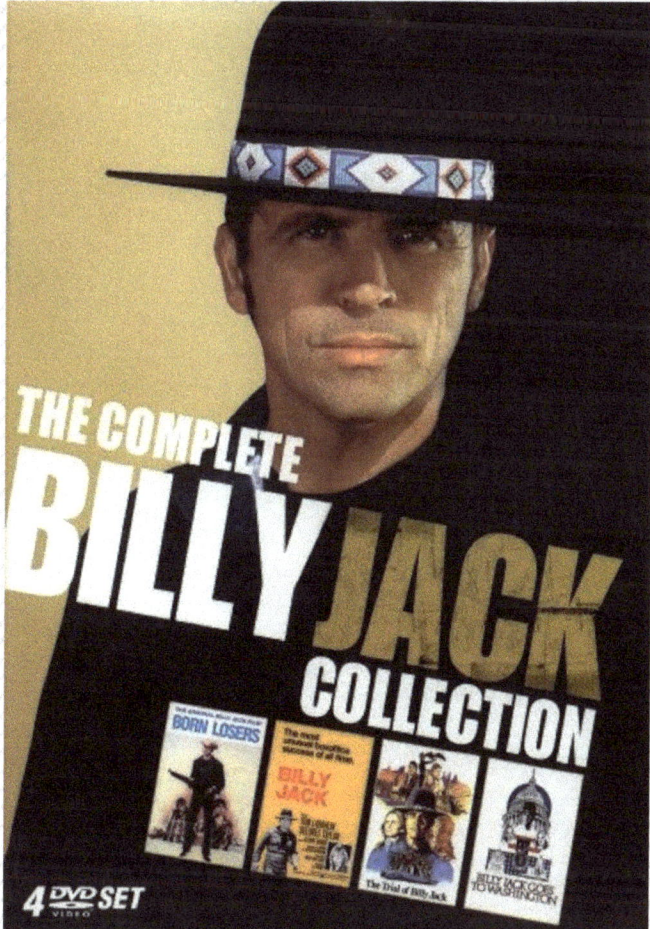

cut corners, tied together shots, got things for free, made things look more expensive than they were....... Seriously, it comes off more like the bonus features on a Robert Rodriguez DVD (just without the cooking recipes.) Its obvious that Mr. Laughlin and Ms. Taylor wanted to encourage others to pick up the baton they had carried so far on their own. If you want to make movies, do yourself a favor and give it ALL a good listen! You're welcome.

About the Author:
Jason McNeil is an actor, writer and martial artist who has appeared in numerous movies and television shows, including as host of Stars-Stunts-Action! - taking you behind the scenes of action movies and martial arts entertainment! - now streaming on Tubi!

吴京
WU JING
From Hong Kong Hopeful to Mainland Hero
By Paul Bramhall

It's been over 25 years since Wu Jing debuted on Hong Kong cinema screens in 1996's Tai Chi Boxer, a production which saw him billed as the next Jet Li thanks to their shared history of being on the Beijing Wushu Team. While it's debatable exactly what criteria would need to be ticked off in order to fulfil the prediction of being the next Jet Li, what can't be argued is that over the course of his career, Jing would come to re-invent himself almost every 10 years on the dot. A mix of his own ambitions equally combined with the climate of the times, the reasons behind each reinvention ranged from the commercial to the political, making him one of the most intriguing members of what can be considered the last batch of legitimate martial arts stars.

As of the time of writing Jing is one of the most bankable stars in China, headlining the top 2 highest grossing Chinese productions of all time – 2021's The Battle at Lake Changjin in first place, closely followed by his self-directed 2017 sequel Wolf Warrior 2 in second. Having conquered China, earlier this year he got to flex his muscles in Hollywood by co-starring alongside Jason Statham in Meg 2: The Trench, and while we were robbed of any kung-fu versus megalodon action, his appearance in a Hollywood blockbuster further cements his presence on the world stage.

For someone who for many years was considered as the guy who just couldn't catch the break he deserved, as he approaches his 50th year things can certainly be said to have worked out in the end. The most interesting aspect to Wu Jing's ascension to box office stardom, is that it's taken a very different path from what many of the fans who were introduced to him in the 1990's or 2000's would have expected. In this feature, we'll take a look at what I like to call the 3 seasons

of Wu Jing. Why only 3? With Jing's stardom showing no signs of abating, chances are the 4th season is still to come.

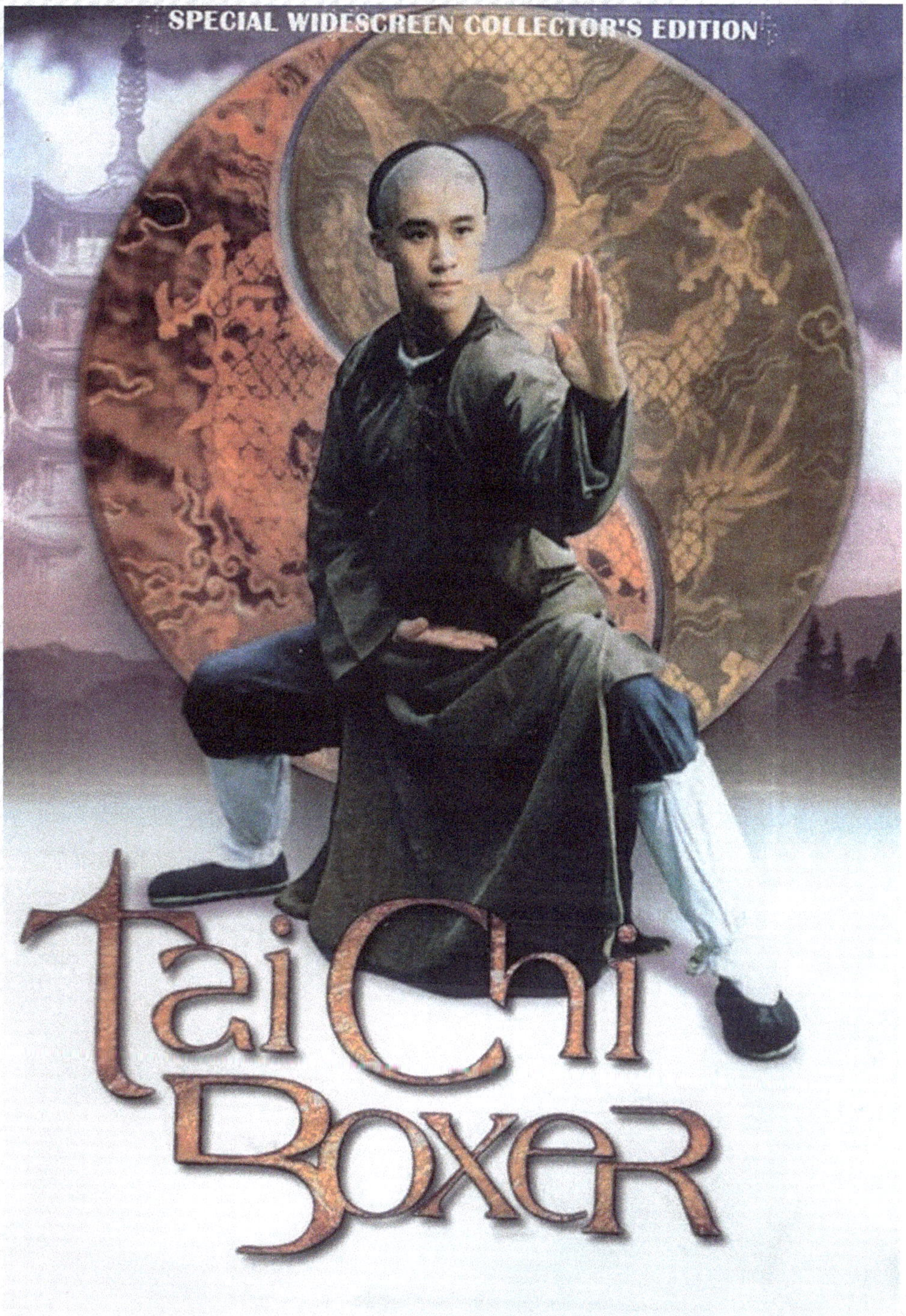

Winter: Beginnings – 1996 to 2004

At a time when Hong Kong was just a year away from being handed back to China, most of the territories biggest stars had jumped ship for Hollywood, and the traditional kung-fu movie had long fallen out of fashion, director Yuen Woo-Ping decided to debut his latest discovery Wu Jing in 1996's Tai Chi Boxer (which notably in some territories was released as Tai Chi II, billing it as a sequel to the Jet Li starring Tai Chi Master from 1993). Casting an unfamiliar face to be the star in a genre that was no longer flavor of the month may have been risky, but what can't be denied is that as a leading man the 21-year-old Jing delivered a likable charm, topped off by an impressive screen fighting pedigree that showed he was the real deal. Busting out the moves against gweilo new blood like Darren Shahlavi and the ever-dependable Billy Chow, under the choreography of Woo-Ping everyone delivered top shelf action performances.

Regardless of how solid a kung-fu movie Tai Chi Boxer was though, it was never destined to set the box office alight, so it was no surprise when it didn't. Despite this, the same way that Woo-Ping was responsible for launching the career of Donnie Yen in the previous decade (and remained working with him up until just a couple of years prior to Tai Chi Boxer with 1994's Wing Chun), for a moment it looked like the legendary choreographer was going to make Wu Jing his new muse into the 2000's. A couple of years after Tai Chi Boxer, with the kung-fu movie no longer a viable proposition, the pair would reunite for the 28-episode Mainland TV martial arts drama The Tai Chi Master (which was released as an edited down version in the U.S. on DVD by Tai Seng).

Barring the distinct low quality made for TV look that Mainland series from this era came with, Woo-Ping once more offered up a solid showcase for Jing's skills, even if the proposition of both of their talents being relegated to working in the Mainland TV arena certainly wasn't an appealing one. As it happened, the proposition would prove to be an unfounded one, but unfortunately only for one of them – and it wasn't Wu Jing. A relatively unknown Hollywood directing duo by the name of the (formerly known as) Wachowski Brothers called upon Woo-Ping to travel to the U.S. and not only choreograph a little heard of movie called The Matrix they were working on, but also put the cast through an intensive screen fighting training program prior to rolling the camera. It was a unique opportunity, and one that Woo-Ping understandably said yes to, and as a result Jing was left blowing in the wind.

Without the opportunity to develop the same lasting relationship with the legendary choreographer that Donnie Yen was gifted with, and with seemingly no avenues back to Hong Kong, Jing would go on to carve out a career for himself in Mainland TV martial arts series. Throughout the 2000's he'd play the starring role or one of the main characters in 8 such series (and supporting roles in several more), with names like Shaolin King of Martial Arts (2002), 36th Chamber of Southern Shaolin (2004), and Wu Dang (2005). It was only when Woo-Ping returned to Hong Kong after The Matrix finished production that Jing would once more return to HK cinema screens, however it was no longer in a leading role, instead playing a supporting character in Tsui Hark's 2001 sequel The Legend of Zu opposite fellow Beijinger Zhang Ziyi.

Jing's role in The Legend of Zu offered up one of the rare instances for some grounded action in the special effects heavy spectacle, as Woo-Ping choreographed a sword fight between Jing and Ziyi (who Woo-Ping also reunited with after working together on the previous years Crouching Tiger, Hidden Dragon). While an auteur like Tsui Hark had created some of the defining works of fellow martial artists like Jet Li (Once Upon a Time in China I – III) and Vincent Zhao (The Blade, Green Snake) in the previous decade, it appeared like Jing's appearance was likely called in thanks to Woo-Ping's involvement rather than Hark finding a new martial arts muse. In fact it'd take 20 years for the pair to collaborate again with 2021's The Battle at Lake Changjin, and next time it'd be Wu Jing who'd be the megastar, while Hark found himself co-directing a Mainland targeted war movie alongside Chen Kaige and Dante Lam.

In the early 2000's it may have looked like Jing was set to be a Mainland TV series mainstay with only supporting roles on offer in Hong Kong productions, but in 2003 fortune would

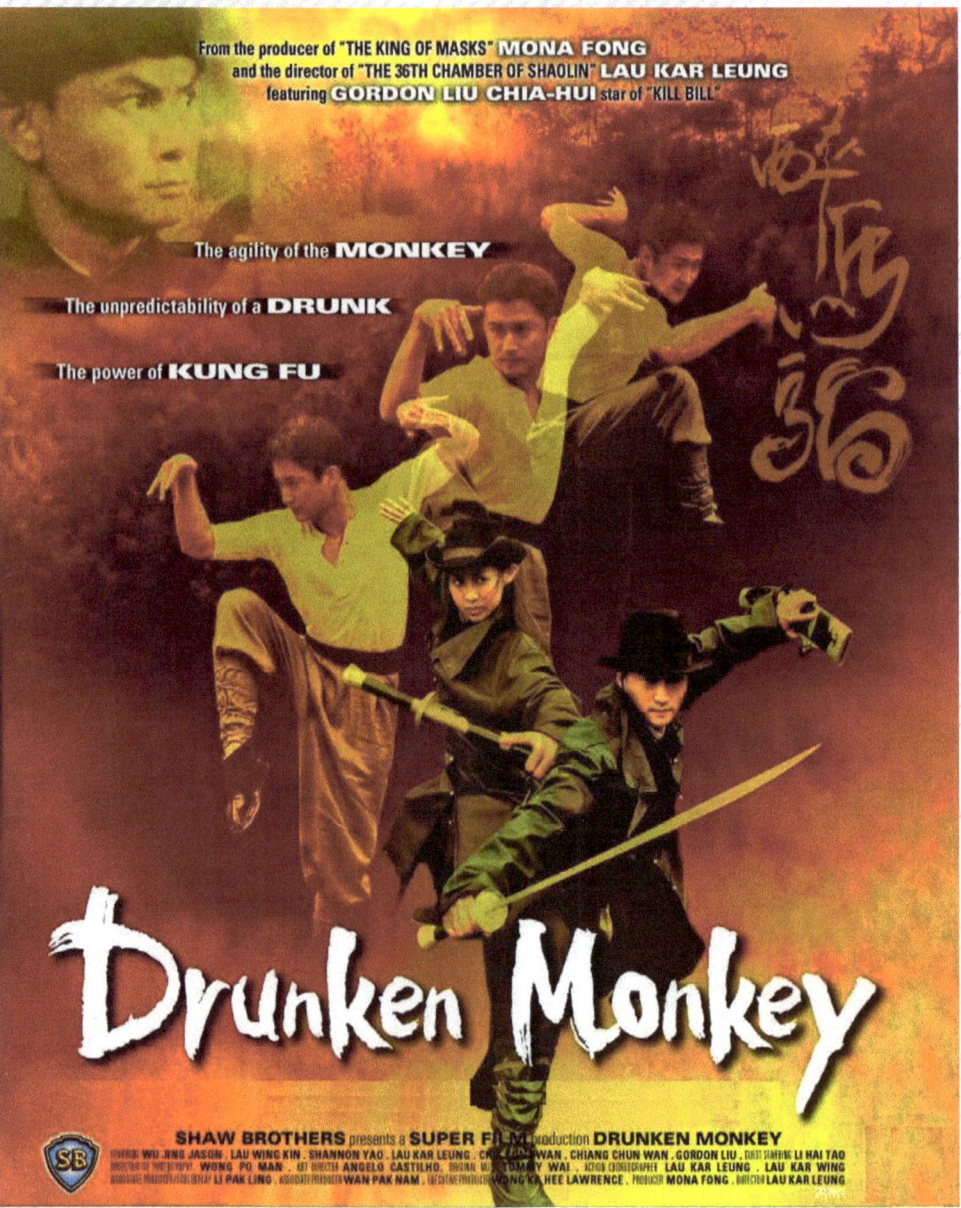

shine on him once more. Not only were the legendary Shaw Brothers studio looking to resume film production for the first time since 1997's Hero, it was also announced that Lau Kar-Leung was returning to both direct and appear in front of the camera for the first time in almost a decade. The project became Drunken Monkey, and was intended to be a throwback to the traditional kung-fu movies of the 70's, all they needed was a star who could pull off the moves without the need for camera trickery or CGI – enter Wu Jing. Taking the starring role and backed up by Shaw Brothers legends like Gordon Liu and Chen Kuan-Chun, Jing essentially stepped into the role that Hsiao Ho played in Mad Monkey Kung Fu 24 years earlier, making his casting a no-brainer.

I'm sure the distributors and marketing team did their best to glaze over the fact that, while Kar-Leung hadn't been active in the film industry for almost a decade, the last time he was resulted in 1994's lamentable Drunken Master III. Sadly, Drunken Monkey turned out to be much closer to Kar-Leung's last outing than it did any of his 70's classics. Jing puts in a commendable performance, however Kar-Leung's rust in the director's chair is apparent, stuffing the runtime with grating comedy and a generic plot that struggles to maintain the audience's attention. The subsequent box office failure of Drunken Monkey scared the Shaw Brothers off from movie production almost as quickly as they'd returned, and now 7 years since Jing's debut in Tai Chi Boxer, it seemed to mark the final nail in the coffin for those hoping that he'd finally catch the break his talents deserved.

Spring: Renaissance – 2005 to 2014

It's often said that if you want a different outcome, sometimes all you need to do is look at the problem from a different perspective. After 7 years of playing the good guy, it would be 2005 that gave audiences a new perspective

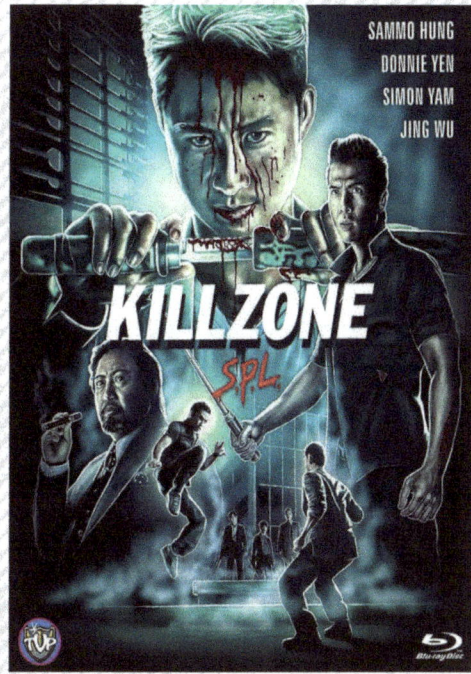

on Wu Jing – one that saw him as a villain. Director Wilson Yip's Sha Po Lang (or Kill Zone as it was tragically re-titled to in the U.S.) proved to be a significant Hong Kong movie in more ways than one. After loitering around in supporting roles the previous year, SPL would mark the first starring role in a HK production for Donnie Yen since his trio of self-directed features made across 1997 and 1998, and his return saw him as a man on a mission. With 2003's Thai action breakout Ong Bak leaving the once renowned HK action scene in the dust, Yen wanted to make a movie that would put it back on the map, and SPL was intended to be it.

Despite the 3 stars in Chinese astrology that the title Sha Po Lang refers to being represented by Yen, Sammo Hung, and Simon Yam, it was Jing's turn as Sammo Hung's righthand man that led to the productions most memorable scene – an alleyway fight between Jing and Yen that precedes the finale. Consisting of a dagger brandishing Jing facing off against an extendable police baton wielding Yen, the fight is rightly regarded as an all-time classic. Fast, brutal, and containing moments of spontaneous choreography only possible through having 2 martial artists performing at the top of their game, the image of the white suited Jing and his shock of blonde dyed hair was a revelation. The fight itself was parodied 15 years later in Donnie Yen's Enter the Fat Dragon, with Philip Ng stepping into Jing's role, and is guaranteed to come up in any discussion on greatest fight scenes to grace the screen.

Jing's role proved to the breakthrough he'd been looking for, and over the course of the next 9 years he'd turn up in a total of

Celina Jade, who ends up in peril once the gangsters move in to take revenge for their boss being killed. Interestingly the finale seems to take a cue from The Matrix Revolutions, with Jing forced to take on dozens of identically dressed attackers during a rain-soaked night setting, choosing to rely heavily on his kicking skills more than wushu, which gives it a distinctly different feel than his usual approach to action. Legendary Assassin definitely didn't set the box office alight, and was far from being a strong debut from a directorial perspective, factors which would result in Jing sticking to being in front of the camera for the rest of the decade.

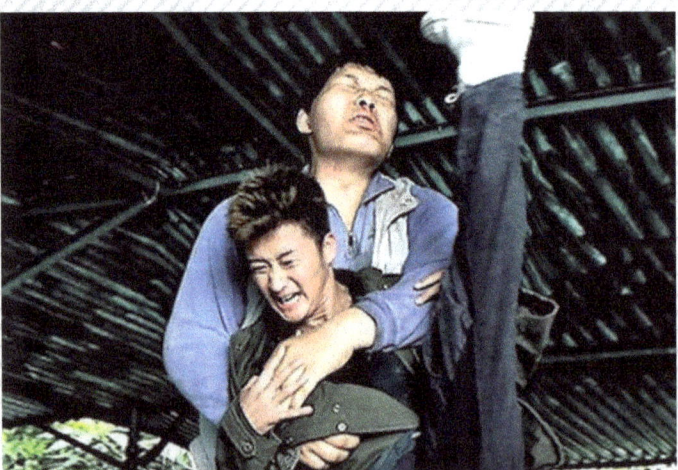

It was during the promotional period for Legendary Assassin that Jing got himself embroiled in some controversy with the Hong Kong martial arts community, specifically wing chun practitioners. When asked about the dispute that was ongoing at the time as to whose production should have the right to be called Ip Man – Wilson Yip or Wong Kar Wai – both of whom had movies about the wing chun masters life that (at the time – in reality Kar Wai's movie would take another 5 years to be released) were due out in 2008, Jing responded "I first learned this name from the press about the conflict in the filming of the life of Ip Man. I thought, 'Who is this man that there is such a fuss about?'" His apparent ignorance of Ip Man caused offence to producer and wing chun master Sin Kwok Lam, who challenged Jing to fight against either Dennis To (who would ironically go on to play Ip Man himself 2 years later) or Vivi Lee, a wing chun exponent.

Ultimately nothing came of the challenge, and Jing's offending of certain parts of the Hong Kong community was perhaps a timely one. With China going through an economic boom the cinematic landscape was beginning to change in the late 00's, with hundreds of multiplexes being built thanks to a burgeoning middle class who loved to go the cinema. It wasn't long before Hollywood got smart to the fact that a movies box office potential could be increased dramatically by appealing to a Chinese audience, and it was from this line of thinking that the China-Hollywood co-production was born. These late 2000's to mid-2010's productions, made before relations between the 2 countries deteriorated, would typically look like big budget Hollywood productions on the surface, but came with significant Chinese investment towards the budget.

The trade-off meant that Chinese stars usually showed up in in supporting roles, and typically parts of the movie would find an excuse to take place in China, all of which meant box office appeal for both sides. Such was the case for the third entry in The Mummy franchise, titled The Mummy: Tomb of the Dragon Emperor. While Brendan Fraser and co. spend most of their time dealing with the emperor of the title, played by another wushu luminary in the form of Jet Li, here Jing gets a brief role as an assassin, offering up his first appearance in a big budget Hollywood franchise. As a related sidenote, in 2013 Marvel's Iron Man 3 would also be a co-production between Hollywood and China, and Jing shot an action scene which was intended to be shown in the China distributed version of the production, but ultimately would become missing in action from all known prints. Call it Wu Jing's very own saw in the head scene!

Prior to 2008, in the same year as Twins Mission Jing would return on villain duty in Benny Chan's action flick Invisible Target. A big budget starring vehicle for the trio of Nicholas Tse, Shawn Yu, and Jaycee Chan, it gave Jing his most mainstream exposure yet in terms of prominent roles. Once more paired with choreographer Nicky Li, the action wisely pays respect to his martial arts talents by needing all 3 of the protagonist's team up in order to take him out during the satisfyingly action-packed finale. Invisible Target would see Jing go on to appear in

several of Benny Chan's productions, usually in memorable supporting roles, including 2010's City Under Siege and 2011's Shaolin.

For City Under Siege in particular, while arguably the most insufferable title in all of Benny Chan's filmography, the pairing of Jing and Zhang Jingchu as mutant hunting Mainland cops provides the sole reason to check it out. Their scenes offer a glimmer of what the production should have been, agents equipped with superior kung-fu skills ready to unleash them onto any unsuspecting mutant criminal at a moment's notice, but as it is they play 2nd fiddle to a horrendously handled romance between Aaron Kwok and Shu Qi. On the other hand, while Shaolin offered up not 1 but 2 of likely every up-and-coming martial arts stars dreams – being choreographed by Corey Yuen, and getting to feature alongside Jackie Chan – Jing's role feels mostly perfunctory in much the same way it was 10 years prior in Tsui Hark's The Legend of Zu. The rise of the Mainland film industry would offer up the opportunity for Jing to start shifting away from Hong Kong, and 3 years after his (unintentionally) controversial comments about Ip Man, in 2010 he released a lengthy statement on the now defunct wujing.org site. In it he expressed his woes about working in HK by saying he was "hiding behind one after another new set of clothes playing a nice Hong Kong lad over a long time, I feel that I have lost my bearing." Revealing that he'd been offered the lead role of a soldier in a military themed Chinese TV drama, he went on to explain his conflicts around the "distinction between movie stars and TV stars", concluding that it's been his "wish to be soldier since young, and now I have a chance to act as a solider, what's there to hesitate? Why bother if it's a movie or TV series, as long as you get a chance to covey the artistic image you wish…" The lead role being referred to was in 2012's Special Arms, but prior to taking it on Jing was already starting to pop up in an increasing number of Mainland productions, with supporting roles in the likes of 2010's Wind Blast (a rare Mainland attempt at a HK style action flick) and the comedy Love Tactics. The trend would continue by appearing opposite Jet Li again in 2013's Badges of Fury (a co-production with Hong Kong) and 2014's The Breakup Guru. With the benefit of hindsight, Jing's presence in Hong Kong productions around the same time was also noticeably decreasing, with throwaway roles in the likes of 2009's Metallic Attraction: Kungfu Cyborg, 2010's Just Another Pandora's Box and 2011's Magic to Win being indicative of a performer who'd lost the passion he so obviously had during that golden 2005 – 2008 period.

By 2014 Wu Jing's course seemed to be set - finding contentment in headlining Chinese TV action dramas, marrying his partner Xie Nan (who he featured alongside in The Breakup Guru), and continuing to appear in supporting roles in local Mainland productions. Almost 20 years since his debut he'd built up a respectable body of work, even if many would say he never really got the big break he deserved like his contemporaries Jet Li and Donnie Yen. However with his roles in the likes of Sha Po Lang and Fatal Contact, Jing was at least going to be remembered as a solid screen fighter who always delivered, and the alley way fight in the former will always be mentioned as one of the greatest fight scenes to be put on film. Wu Jing may have finished this era by turning his back on the Hong Kong celebrity lifestyle, but he left behind a solid body of work that we can always enjoy, and nothing can change that.

Summer: Ascension – 2015 to Present

Purely from the perspective of being a kung-fu movie star, reaching the peak of your career once you're over 40 is practically unheard of, however Wu Jing had other ideas. Initially this period of Jing's career looked like he may not be turning his back on the Hong Kong film industry after all, as 10 years since his iconic role in Sha Po Lang, he was offered the lead role in the thematic sequel, SPL 2: A Time

for Consequences. Paired with Tony Jaa in a Thailand set tale which sees them taking on a corrupt prison warden played by Max Zhang, the sequel gave Jing his first starring role in a Hong Kong production since his self-directed debut Legendary Assassin 7 years earlier. It was worth the wait, as director Soi Cheang brought out a performance in Jing that delivered both on the acting and the action front, leading many to believe that his role could be the breakout fans had been waiting for.

However SPL 2 would turn out to be more of a swansong to his Hong Kong era than a comeback, and while Jing would go on to make a supporting appearance by reuniting with director Benny Chan in the following years Call of Heroes (as well as featuring alongside his wife again in the co-production A Chinese Odyssey: Part 3), it seemed like his time in HK really was over. For his fans it was a double dose of bad news, as not only was he turning his back on what many action cinema fans considered to be the spiritual home of the genre, but he also shared a photo at the time from a hospital bed revealing he'd had surgery on both of his legs.

Despite how things may have looked, in the background it turned out a number of stars were aligning. In 2014 President Xi made his famous (or infamous – depending on your perspective) speech, in which he urged the film industry to make "patriotism the main theme of literary and artistic creation", ushering in the era of the 'main melody' genre. 'Main melody' is an expression used for productions made for the purpose of extolling the virtues of China as a nation, the communist party that rules over it, and of course its military. After Jing's woes of Hong Kong celebrity culture and never being able to catch the break he deserved, the speech seemed to be a rallying call, and he decided to once more step into the director's chair (this time on his home soil) to make what would become 2015's Wolf Warrior.

While there could well be other productions that were released prior to Wolf Warrior, from a popularity perspective, it's widely considered to be the first 'main melody' movie that fully encapsulated President Xi's wishes, essentially being a 90-minute promotion for the awesomeness of the Chinese military. Jing takes the lead role, playing a soldier who's promoted to the Wolf Division, and ultimately has to take on a group of foreign mercenaries planning to make a virus that'll specifically kill Chinese people. The movie itself is a fairly lacklustre affair, even squandering the casting of Scott

Adkins as the villain (not helped by the fact Adkins was carrying an injury at the time), however Wolf Warrior became a production which transcended such details, becoming more about what it represents than whether it's actually good or not.

The overtly jingoistic tone and its complete lack of subtlety may have been jarring for many non-Chinese audiences (this is a movie that closes with an almost 4th wall breaking line of "Those who threaten China's resolve will have no place to hide!"), but in China Wolf Warrior became almost a byword for Chinese pride. Soon the confrontational style of Chinese politics began to be referred to as "wolf warrior diplomacy", with politicians themselves taking pride in being labelled with the moniker, perhaps no more so than Lu Shaye, who became known as the wolf warrior diplomat for his controversial pro-China views. For Jing, after struggling in Hong Kong for so many years, he practically became the face of Chinese pride overnight.

A sequel was immediately green lit, and with almost triple the budget of the original arrived in 2017, somewhat ironically bringing onboard Hollywood talent like Frank Grillo and Sam Hargrave to assist in delivering on the action front. Deliver it did, with Wolf Warrior 2 being a wildly entertaining ride set in Africa (the first of many Chinese movies that would refer to the continent as if it's a country). As much as it elevated the action, so also the jingoistic tones were also cranked up a notch, starting with the movies tagline which literally read "Whoever attacks China will be killed no matter how far the target is." At least they're clear. The sequel ends on a bizarre final scene which simply shows the image of a Chinese passport, along with accompanying text which reads "Citizens of the PRC: When you encounter danger in a foreign land, do not give up! Please remember, at your back stands a strong motherland."

Such scenes may sound like the kind of thing you'd see in a North Korean propaganda movie, and really it's not far from the truth. In March 2018 China's National Radio and Television Administration (NRTA) division, whose role is to approve any content which gets shown on Chinese screens, was transferred to sit under the CCP's Central Propaganda Department. While the move was seen as largely symbolic of what had already been expected from China's film industry since President Xi's 2014 speech, the transfer solidified the expectation that any movie production's primary purpose should be to glorify China, and Jing's Wolf Warrior movies had set the template.

What's most surprising though is that not many propaganda movies are expected to break all box office records, but in China that's exactly what Wolf Warrior 2 did, becoming only the 2nd production in history to reach $800 million in a single territory (the 1st was Star Wars: The Force Awakens in the U.S.). It would go on to knock Stephen Chow's The Mermaid off the top spot, the final nail in the coffin for any last traces of Hong Kong talent having influence on the Mainland box office, and a deluge of movies praising China's military might followed in the succeeding years. From big budget spectacles like Dante Lam's Operation Mekong and Operation Red Sea, to web movies like the Vincent Zhao starring Counterattack and the Wolves Action series, if you wanted your action movie to have a chance of success, a military flick became the go-to genre.

Jing himself had said in his post from 2010 "Farewell, pale face scholar, I want to see, if I could summon a primitive impulsive deep within my heart, could I be a soldier?" His wishes had come true, and after 20 years of attempting to be the next kung-fu superstar, instead Jing finally found the recognition he was seeking through becoming the most recognisable face of China's cinematic propaganda. While immediately after Wolf Warrior 2 he'd clock in a supporting turn in the fantasy comedy The Faces of my Gene (and if we have to mention it, also Alibaba Group founder Jack Ma's bizarre vanity project, the short film On That Night…While We Dream), it quickly became apparent that Jing's role was one of being willingly typecast as the go-to leading man for big budget jingoistic blockbusters.

Across 2019 and 2020 alone Jing would play an Earth saving astronaut in the sci-fi blockbuster Wandering Earth, heroic mountaineer Fang Wuzhou in The Climbers, clock in a supporting role as a soldier in the Korean War set Sacrifice, and lend his name by cameoing in the saccharine My People, My Homeland. While all of these productions were successful on Chinese soil, and for titles like Wandering Earth even gained popularity internationally thanks to a release on Netflix, it was in 2021 that China pulled out all the stops for the mega budget The Battle at Lake Changjin. Like in The Sacrifice the Korean War was once again the setting, this time recounting a pivotal battle in 1950 in which the Chinese forces pushed the US marines back over the 38th parallel. Doesn't a movie set in the Korean War at least need some Koreans in it, be they actors or at least characters? Apparently not when you're China.

Commissioned by the Central Propaganda Department as part of the CCP's 100th anniversary celebrations, the government threw a mind-boggling budget of $200 million to bring the story to the screen, hiring fifth generation filmmaker Chen Kaige, action maestro Dante Lam, and Hong Kong auteur Tsui Hark to direct. Usually a production helmed by any one of the trio was considered a cinematic event, so to have all 3 collaborating on the same movie was an exciting proposition. The fact that it had to be a propaganda war flick, one created to celebrate the communist parties 100th anniversary, understandably resulted in plenty of mixed feelings from the directors fanbases. Of course, there was only one choice for the lead role – Wu Jing. Expectedly, The Battle at Lake Changjin broke all box office records in China, surpassing Jing's own Wolf Warrior 2, and was swiftly followed by a filmed back-to-back sequel in 2022.

25 years after making his debut in Tai Chi Boxer, Jing found himself as the star of China's 2 highest grossing movies of all time, meaning it's perfectly possible that audiences

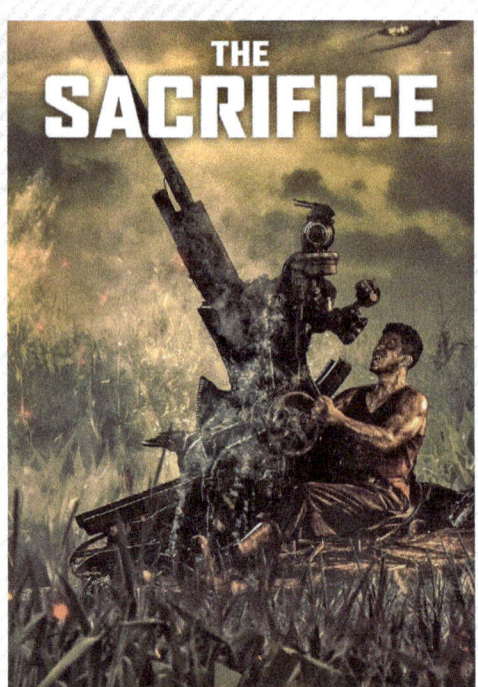

just discovering him will be completely unaware that he was once one of the most promising talents in Hong Kong's kung-fu genre. The success of The Battle at Lake Changjin once more reaffirmed Jing's status as being China's premier star, and in 2023 he'd step up to again headline the sequel to Wandering Earth, which is notable because I'm sure not even Jing himself ever thought he'd take top billing over his HK legend co-star Andy Lau. Jing's role in Wandering Earth 2 means that he's in half of the top 10 highest grossing Chinese movies of all time (the other 2 being the original and The Battle at Lake Changjin II), his appearance practically being a guarantee of success.

Almost becoming an omnipresent fixture in big budget Chinese cinema, in 2022 he'd also cameo in the Chinese citizen evacuation thriller Homecoming (hopefully the characters in this one took note of Wolf Warrior 2's passport featuring last scene), and take on a supporting role playing a coach in

the 2023 sporting drama Ping Pong: The Triumph. Surprisingly, the Jackie Chan starring drama Ride On offered up a rare non-jingoistic supporting turn for Jing, perhaps as a nod of acknowledgement to his kung-fu days. What's next for Jing in the ever-shifting world of Chinese cinema remains to be seen. In 2017 the closing moments of Wolf Warrior 2 assured us that Wolf Warrior 3 would be coming soon, however 6 years later there's zero trace of it.

One theory can be derived from looking at the approach we've seen in the likes of The Climbers, Wandering Earth, and The Battle at Lake Changjin, wherein it seems like the one person as the hero approach has fallen out of favor with the CCP. Now it's all about ensemble pieces, where victory is only guaranteed if all Chinese people unite together behind the common good, meaning the place for the solo Wolf Warrior in the current cinematic environment is no longer a viable one when emphasising the united Chinese spirit. Whatever the case may be, Jing has proven to be flexible with the times, perhaps none more so than his latest appearance alongside Jason Statham in The Meg 2: The Trench, pitting China and America's finest against the toothy terror of multiple megalodons. As Jing's first primarily English language role, I'm sure it'll only result in his popularity continuing to rise.

Unleashing the Magic of Asian Cinema

Interview with Cedric Behrel
Director of Trinity CineAsia

SP: In 2016, Trinity Filmed Entertainment took over CineAsia. What inspired Trinity to run the label the return to release new films?

CB: I personally have always been in love with Asian cinema, starting with the action legends I came across in the dark corners of video stores, the same films that attract premium prices now! Back then, they sat alongside shock-horror and the latest Cronenberg. I was a big fan of Bruce Lee as a child, but also the likes of Tsui Hark and Chow Yun Fat growing up. I was finding these films under the radar, thanks to my cinephile, benevolent granddad Bernard who gave me a lot of freedom, shall we say, at the video store. In France, the certification policy for video (and film too) was much more relaxed then the BBFC. Bernard is the one who introduced me to Bruce Lee and showed me The Killer. Pretty cool for a granddad!

Then I really came of age with the so-called fifth generation Chinese filmmakers like Zhang Yimou and Chen Kaige, whose work I saw in the cinema. Again, I was underage but I knew the London cinemas pretty well in terms of where you could see a '15' certificate without too much trouble and where it was possible to go in and see an '18' rated film with an adult! This followed with discovering Wong Kar Wai who dazzled me when I started university and the Japanese new wave of the 1990s; Kitano, Kyoshi, Kurosawa, Takashi Miike and also the early films of Park Chan-Wook, Jang Sun-Woo and Kim Ki-Duk. I discovered Ichi The Killer after an early trip to Tokyo and, having stayed in Shinjuku, it seemed like a (very) dark echo of that experience.

Really it was a commercial decision at the time, but I think the inspiration to take over the label came from there.

SP: As a recent highlight, Trinity CineAsia released Raging Fire in late 2021, which was Benny Chan's final film before he passed, starring Donnie Yen and Nicholas Tse. The 4K Ultra HD steelbook is beautiful. And do you plan to re-release any Special Edition double disc sets in the future?

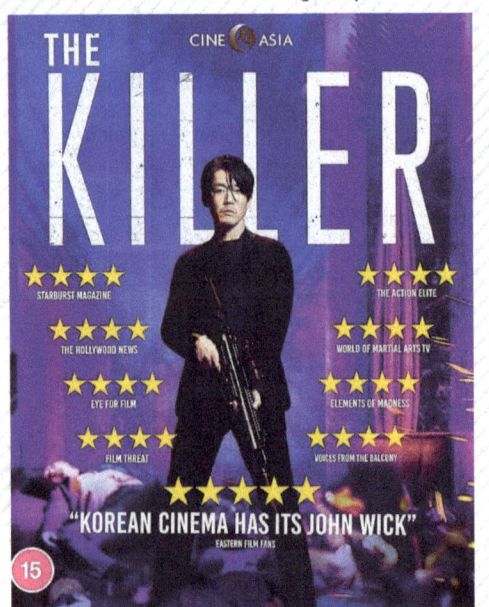

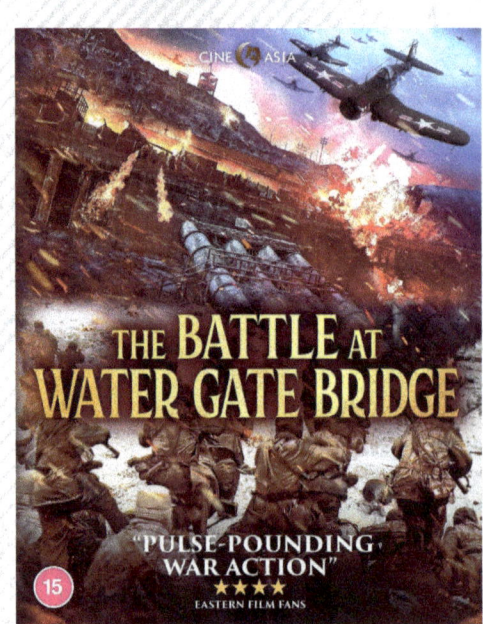

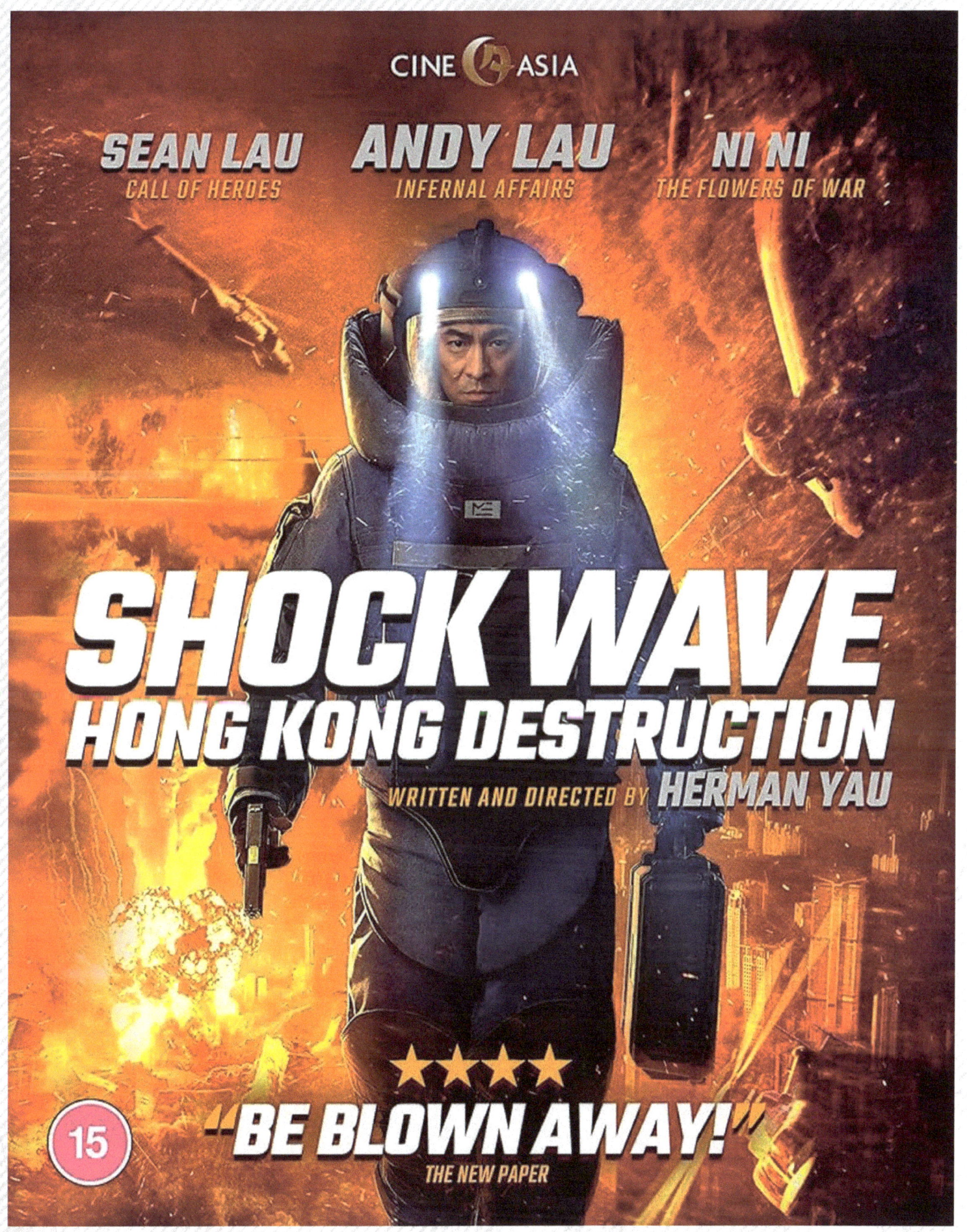

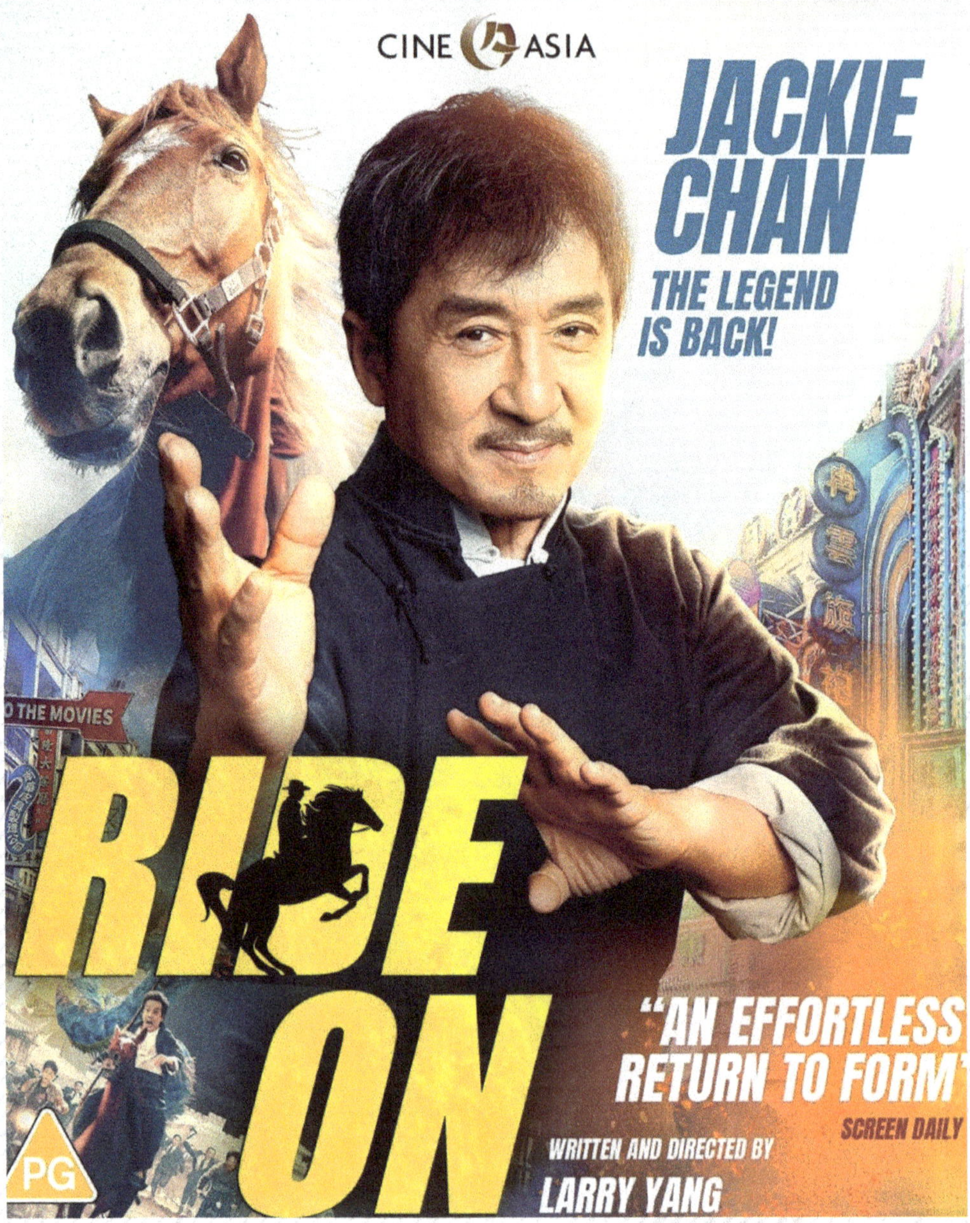

CB: Thank you and we're very proud of releasing Raging Fire which is an exceptional film, and we're happy to have released several other films from the late Benny Chan. I'm not sure double-discs are that necessary in our current time but special editions, definitely. We do have plans, yes, but before I can reveal anything I think we should do a consultation process with fans, such as you readers!

In fact, we are always looking for physical media enthusiasts to help us with our library going forward, and you can consider an open call for submissions and suggestions!

SP: Due to competition with streaming services and the additional costs associated with physical media, does this limit the ability for production and especially the more niche collectible Special Edition Blu-ray box-sets, for example?

CB: Not really, I believe there is and always will be a place for high-end physical media releases. The question is: at what cost? To be honest, it's not something we have been totally focused on due to our expansion in other corners of Asian cinema and our concentration on expanding cinema releases and video-on-demand in other territories as well. And it seems, at the moment, to mostly be the domain of 2K/4K re-issues of classics, which is not really our realm. However, this is not to say we won't. In fact, we do have plans in that space, under wraps for now.

SP: While other Asian cinema labels seem to focus on restoration and re-releases of classic films, Trinity CineAsia is unique in releasing contemporary Asian films in the West, with recent highlights including Korean John Wick style thriller The Killer, sci-fi blockbuster The Wandering Earth II and Jackie Chan's latest film, Ride On. How have you achieved this?

CB: It comes down to relationships and trust acquired over the years, consolidated over many trips to Asia, plus film festivals and markets. The legacy of the CineAsia label certainly helped by way of introduction. Then we worked hard to keep these relationships going, and constantly following up. It doesn't mean we will get everything we want all the time, but we keep working at it.

SP: Eastern cinema is such a huge subject with such a variety of genres. From Miike having a guy in a frog costume kicking ass in Yakuza Apocalypse to the high-school fairy tale Secret by Jay Chou, which is beautiful and magically shot. How do you decide which films you release?

CB: Yes I love that film! Still puzzled by it. Wasn't Yakuza Apocalypse one of the weirdest films ever? Part of deciding what we release is relationships, part of it is creating your own opportunities (and seizing them) and part of it is marketing analysis and knowledge,

trying to understand audiences' tastes and preferences. We constantly explore what is being made and released, and what we think our audience would like to see. We are lucky enough to see materials before everyone else, be it early scenes, promos or scripts, so this can help steer us and get inspired.

SP: Your new releases this year include Jackie Chan's latest film, Ride On, which felt like a real throwback and return to form. You also released Born to Fly, which is an epic action film drawing comparisons to Top Gun! Do you do any special promotional activity for these types of releases?

CB: Yes, absolutely! We have a marketing team working hard at it. We always try to keep some nice surprises, like Jackie Chan doing a special shout out for his UK fans, who obviously have a long history supporting his work.

Born to Fly was an amazing film to bring to cinemas, with its impressive aerial sequences and superb, immersive sound mix. It was stunning on the big screen and we equally can't wait to bring this to home entertainment formats later in the year, especially good for those with 55" screens and Dolby Atmos at home!

SP: Are there any films you are hoping to release in the future you can tell us about?

CB: Yes, there are a few Hong Kong films we're excited about, and we also have home entertainment releases incoming, starting with Ride On, The Wandering Earth II and Born to Fly. Later in the year we're planning to bring you something exciting on the big screen. Not to forget 4k – more on this soon.

SP: What is the long-term vision for Trinity CineAsia?

CB: In a way, it's the same it's always been, to bring you some of the most exciting films to come out of Asia, across the unique mix of storytelling, genre, epic scale, mind-blowing action, all-out fantasy and a certain form of nostalgia.

Asia has grown a lot in the past few years, it is still expanding and I'm confident that it will continue to deliver outstanding cinema. It's also the continent of major change par excellence. Everything seems to be in permanent flux, yet they are constant threads that never go away, and you learn to recognize more every time you go back. But you never know what it will throw at you.

I would say you can expect more variety, especially in cinemas, which is something I would like to extend as well to video-on-demand and home entertainment. But it's also proving tricky; the whole industry has seen physical sales eroding, with some stores deciding to de-stock physical media, the DVD format in decline and audience fragmentation on video-on-demand, with viewers being pulled apart by streamer wars over original content. So it's not necessarily easy to operate in this field nowadays, which is why I think a lot of labels are shifting to re-releasing classics. We admire that approach and the loving restorations many of these films get, however we want to remain active in new releases and work with exciting new and active filmmakers. There are many opportunities, and my feeling is that we need to engage with passionate audiences to start a dialogue about what we want to see and where.

SP Thank you for speaking with us. It has been a pleasure. We cannot wait for more of your releases and wish you all the best.

Please visit Trinity CineAsia at www.trintycineasia.com or check them out on Facebook, Instagram, Twitter, Weibo and YouTube or scan the QR code below.

FANATICAL DRAGON PRESENTS
5 FINGERS OF DISCS

By Johnny Burnett

Greetings once again dear friends, the last few years has seen a huge push for Shaw Brothers movies making their transition onto the Bluray format with more and more labels jumping onto the Shaw's bandwagon (or rickshaw maybe?) and giving us new releases of well known classics as well as a fair few titles that are more obscure. Let's take a look together at some of the more recent releases, for ease I'll divide them into sections grouped by the boutique label which has released them..

Arrow Video

Arrow have been delivering the highest quality releases in terms of titles and presentation these past few years, their two Shawscope boxsets (volume 1 & 2) offer up 24 movies split over two sets, jam packed with extras and they've included a huge number of fan favourites in terms of title selections, A third Volume is lined up for 2024 with potentially a forth to follow in 2025. Arrow have indicated Volume 3 will move away from Kung FU movies into other areas of Shaw's extensive back catalogue, my money would be on Horror, Wu Xia/Fantasy and likely crime dramas, but time will tell, for now, the sets they have already delivered, remain THE most definitive Shaw Brother's releases available anywhere…..

ShawScope Volume 1
Bluray
Region A (US)
Region B (UK)
Out of Print (replaced with three smaller sets in regular packaging, see below for more info)

The first Shawscope Boxset (Blue Box) launched Arrow firmly into pole position in the race amongst the boutique bluray labels to put out Shaw Brothers titles, thanks largely to the company's ability to secure the rights to several really big titles, Volume 1 was almost entirely focused on the work of Chang Cheh and Lau Kar Leung (for obvious reasons) Volume One contained remastered versions of 12 Shaw's movies: Five Fingers of Death Aka King Boxer, The Boxer From Shantung, Five Shaolin Masters, Shaolin Temple, Mighty Peking Man, Challenge Of The Masters, Executioners from Shaolin, The Chinatown Kid, Five Deadly Venoms, Crippled Avengers, Heroes of The East and Dirty Ho Extras were superb, a mountain of archival interviews with Shaw's actors from Frederic Ambroisine's archives as well as a host of newly created content, custom artwork for each movie, audio commentaries from Terrance J Brady, Jonathan Clements, David Desser and Travis Crawford, Video Essays from Tony Rayns, trailers, image galleries and documentaries. it all added up to a mammoth set, I reviewed this set disc by disc over on my youtube channel for anyone interested in a deep dive into each film and disc from the boxset…

ShawScope Volume 2
Bluray
Region A (US)
Region B (UK)

Volume Two (Red Box) kept the focus firmly on classic Kung Fu and in particular Chang Cheh and Lau Kar Leung and added even more really popular classics to the Arrow lineup it also upped the number of the movies included to 14 films on the set.. It included all three 36th Chamber of Shaolin movies (the original, return to the 36th chamber and disciples of the 36th chamber) Mad Monkey Kung Fu, Five Superfighters, Invincible Shaolin, The Kid With The Golden Arm, Magnificent Ruffians, 10 Tigers of Kwantung, My Young Auntie, Mercenaries from Hong Kong, Boxer's Omen, Martial Arts of Shaolin and The Bare Footed Kid.

Both Volume 1 and 2 also included 2 Audio CD's of music from the De Wolfe music library, which Shaw's had borrowed heavily from when scoring the movies originally.

Volume 2 continued Arrow's quest to provide well produced extra and features a mix of newly produced content and a considerable amount of archive interviews with Shaw's actors and directors from Frederic Ambroisine's archives. mostly filmed in the early 2000's Audio commentaries from Brandon Bentley, Travis Crawford, Frank Djeng, Michael Worth, and Jonathan Clements, video essays from Tony Rayns and more archive and new documentaries. In truth, the Arrow sets are so loaded with extra content, it would take over the entire article to list them all here.

You can check out my breakdown's of Arrow's individual releases of Come Drink With Me and 8 Diagram Pole Fighter below to give you an indication of just how much material they have sourced for these sets…

After the volume one boxset sold out completely, Arrow re-released all the titles from the first boxset into three smaller standalone sets (in standard bluray box sized releases) mostly grouped by director they called these re-release sets 'Shaw Brothers presents'

Shaw Brothers Presents:
Four Films By Chang Cheh
Region A (US)
Region B (UK)
Available Now.

This set contains: Crippled Avengers, Five Deadly Venoms, Five Shaolin Masters and Shaolin Temple with all the on disc extras the movies had on the original Volume 1 Boxset also included.

Shaw Brothers Presents:
Four Films by Lau Kar Leung
Region A (US)
Region B (UK)
Available Now

This groups all the LKL movies from Volume 1 onto one set, Challenge of The Masters, Dirty Ho, Heroes of the East and Executioners from Shaolin. Again retaining all the on-disc extra features from the volume one boxset.

Shaw Brothers Presents:

The Basher Box:
Region A (US)
Region B (UK)
Available Now

This set contains the other Kung Fu movies from the first boxset, The Boxer from Shantung, Chinatown Kid and King Boxer. Mighty Peking Man wasn't included in any of the Shaw Brothers Presents sets, though it is available as a standalone disc from 88 Films (more on that later) Again all on disc extras from the volume 1 boxset are included here…

Arrow also put out two movies as individual, standalone titles in the USA only, both had previously been released in the UK via 88 FIlms, but Arrow were able to secure the US rights and released them both stateside with an incredible array of special features on both. These are both still available direct from Arrow's US website (and shipping to the UK is very cheap!)

Eight Diagram Pole Fighter
Region A (US)

Lau Kar Leung's masterpiece given a new restoration from Arrow themselves and a wealth of incredible extras, a new audio commentary by the wonderful Jonathan Clements, a video introduction from Film critic Tony Rayns, archive interviews with Gorgon Liu and Rita Yeung as well as a short tribute to Alexander Fu Sheng, trailer, image gallery and all new cover

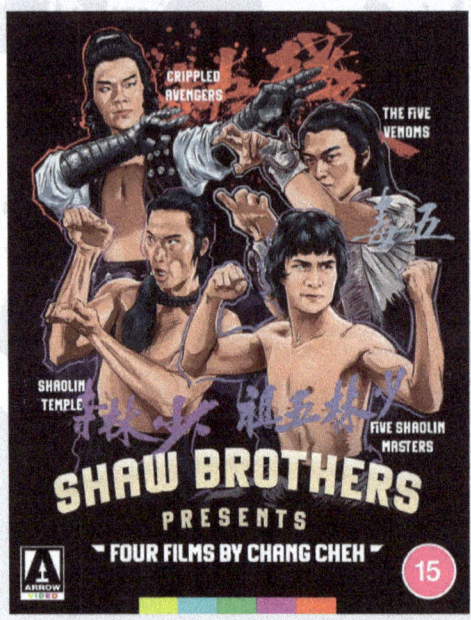

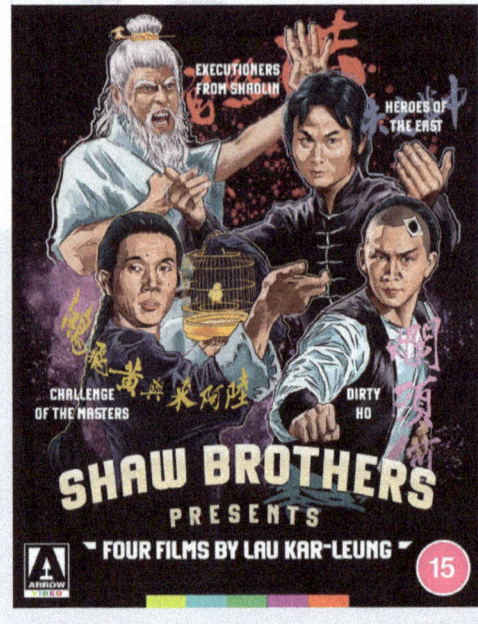

If Arrow is the reigning champion of Shaw's releases worldwide, then next up we have the new challenger looking to take their crown (and ultimately failing, but giving it a damn good try in terms of sheer volume of releases!)

Shout Factory

Shout Factory in the US were late to the party in terms of when they started to put Shaw's titles out, but man have they ever made up for that in terms of quantity in an alarmingly short period of time, in just one year they've put out six boxsets, two of these website exclusives, the other four more widely available, they're much more of a mixed bag than the Arrow releases and rather lacking in extra features, but they've pulled out some quite intriguing titles across the various sets they've put out to date.

Brave Archer Collection
Region A (US)
Shout Website Only

The first set out the gate was The Brave Archer movie series, this was released as a Shout Factory Website exclusive, meaning it was next to impossible to order unless art from Marc Aspinall (with an alternate Arrow website exclusive which featured the original HK poster art on the Slipcover)

Come Drink With Me
Region A (US)

Arrow's other standalone US title was King Hu's Come Drink With me starring the legendary Cheng Pei Pei, again 88 Films had already released this in the UK but Arrow's version pulled in Tony Rayns to record an Audio Commentary (88's version was by Samm Deighan) they also include an interview with star Cheng Pei Pei and Chen Hung Lieh and one part of the mammoth Shaw's documentary series Cinema Hong Kong, an hour long doc focused on the history of the Wu Xia genre and Shaw's contributions to it. Artwork for the release is by the incomparable Tony Stella (again a original HK poster variant was also available via Arrow's US webstore)

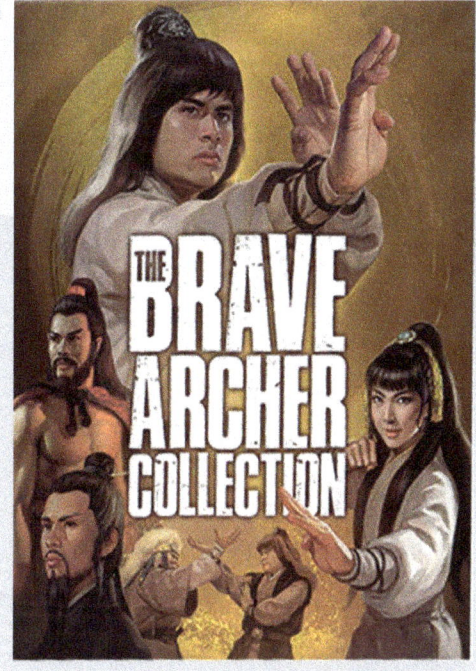

you lived in the USA or Canada, a few US retailers started ordering these in bulk and making them available to customers outside of the USA but shipping and markup costs made this a hell of an expensive boxset all in all (about £50 more than Arrow's Shawscope sets originally retailed at) The Brave Archer Collection brought together, Brave Archer 1, 2 and 3, Brave Archer and His Mate and the Little Dragon Maiden (adapted from the same source material but made much later, wasn't directed by Chang Cheh but did star the late, great Leslie Cheung.) Extras were somewhat lacking when compared to Arrow's outings, but we did get some new documentary and archival interview footage and audio commentaries on two of the films in the series.

Shaw Brothers Classics Volume 1
Region A (US)
Available Now

Shout's first more widely available set, though still limited to the US market, but this was available via Amazon, making shipping to the UK or other parts of the world more cost effective, price was still high, considerably higher than Arrow's boxset, it originally retailed at $170 but tends to sell for around $130 in the US now it's been out for almost a year. The boxset focused on the late 60's era of Wu Xia and early Kung Fu flicks from the studio. The set includes 11 Movies in total: The Assassin, The Thundering Sword, the Golden Swallow, The Jade Raksha, The Bells of Death (easily the best film on the boxset), The Sword of Swords, Killer Dart, The Invincible Fist, Dragon Swamp, The Flying Dagger and The Golden Sword.

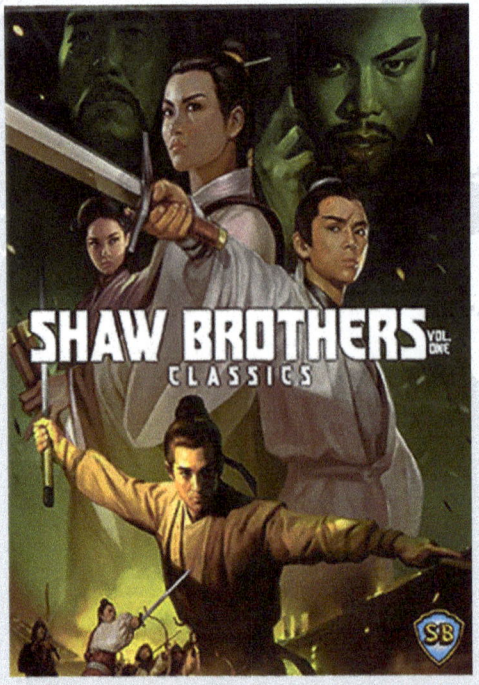

It did up the ante slightly over The Brave Archer set in terms of extras and offered Audio Commentaries on almost every movie, and in some cases, two tracks for a few films, Most are by James Mudge, Gilbert Po, Frank Djeng and Brian Bankston.

Shaw Brothers Classics Volume 2
Region A (US)
Available Now

Arriving less than two months after volume 1, the Vol2 set from Shout moved into the more popular 1970's era of films from the studio and offered up The Lady of Steel, Brothers five, The Crimson Charm, The Shadow whip, The Delightful Forest, The Devils Mirror, Man of Iron, The Water Margin, The Bride From hell, Heroes Two, fan favourite The Flying Guillotine and The Dragon Missile. Again Audio Commentaries are provided for most movies, Tony Rayns provides a video essay on Shaw's horror movies and we get some vintage Celestial Video Extras too.

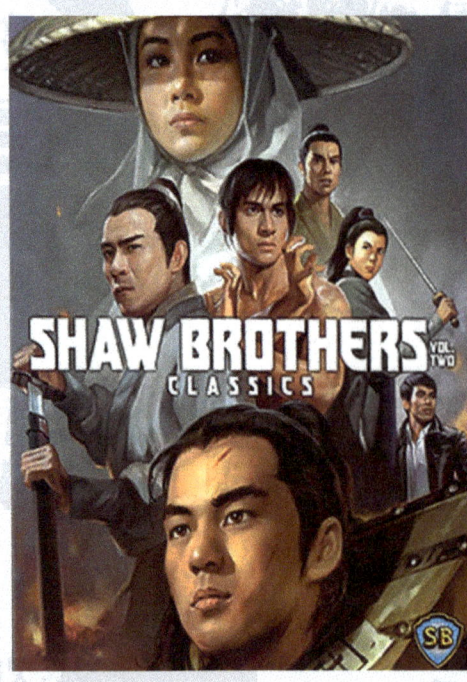

Shaw Brothers Classics Volume 3
Region A (US)
Available Now

Shout kept their relentless pace up and announced Volume 3 before Volume 2 had even been released, it shipped out two months after vol2 and included far more popular and better known films amongst it's line up, Killer Clans, The Shaolin Avengers, the web of Death, The Vengeful Beauty, Death Duel, Life Gamble, Soul of The Sword, the Deadly Breaking Sword, Clan of The white Lotus,

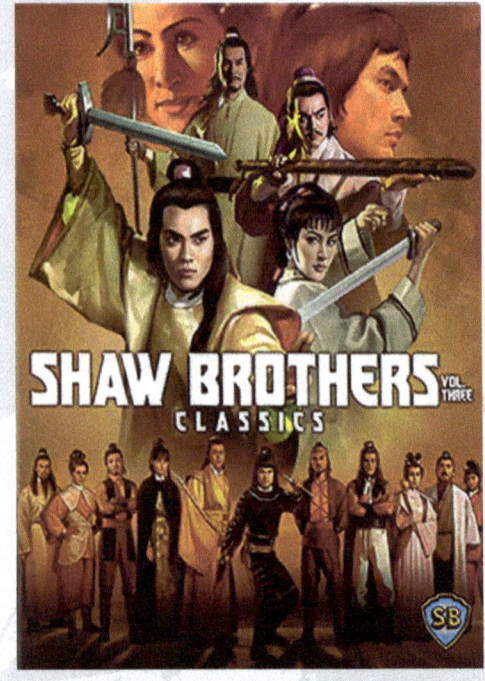

Shaolin Abbot and The Shaolin Rescuers. Extras continued to increase as each set came out and we get lots more video essays alongside the stash of Audio Commentaries on this set.

Shaw Brothers Classics Volume 4
Region A (US)
Available Now

In keeping with their breakneck release schedule, volume 4 was announced just before volume 3 shipped out and included the most popular and most loved movies Shout have put out so far, a very Venom Mob focused set all in all, we get here The Rebel Intruders, Two Champions of Shaolin, Legend of The Fox, Black Lizard, House of Traps, Masked Avengers, The Sword Stained With Royal

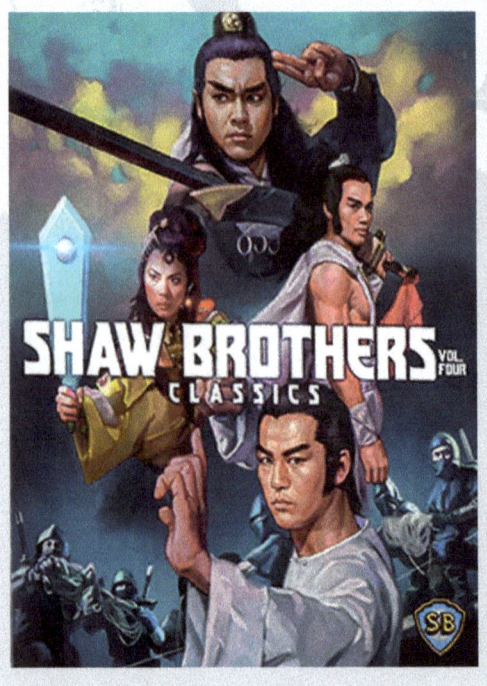

Blood, Five Element Ninja, Shaolin Prince, Shaolin Intruders, Holy Flame of The Martial World and Opium and The Kung Fu Master. This has proved to be the most popular Shout release so far, especially in the US, the selection of films is the most fun (and many of them have never had Bluray releases stateside) The extras are solid, with audio commentaries for most of the movies by a varied roster of commentators and an interview with veteran Shaw's actor Chu Ke split over quite a few of the discs in the boxset.

The Ti Lung / David Chiang Collection
Region A
Available Now
Shout Website Exclusive

The latest (and possibly last) Shout Shaw's release was firmly focused on two major players from the Shaw's acting lineup, Ti Lung and David Chiang and grouped together some of the duo's most well known titles into a 12 movie set. As with the Brave Archer Collection this set is limited to sale only via Shout's own webstore, so is the most expensive of all the Shaw's releases Shout have out out to date, it contains: Have Sword Will Travel, The Heroic ones, Vengeance, the Anonymous Heroes, the Deadly Duo, duel of fists, The Duel, The Angry Guest, All men Are Brothers, The Blood brothers, The Savage Five and 7 man Army. The extras on Shout's set have been steadily increasing as each release comes out, they still pale in comparison to Arrow's incredible efforts, but by the time this Ti Lung/David Chiang set came out, they had arranged an Audio commentary for 11 out of the 12 movies in the box, mostly all by James Mudge from

EasternKicks, with a couple by David West.

All in all it's hard to really rate the overall quality of the Shout releases, they have in a very short period of time, released more titles than any other Boutique label they're up to 65 movies spread over their various boxsets which all came out in one single calendar year, but it's really difficult not to view their efforts as a bit of a cash grab. The quality of Arrow's Two Shawscope boxsets remains the standard by which all other releases are being judged, and thus far nobody has managed to match their level of quality, attention to detail and the care with which they've put together the sets they have released. Whilst the movies themselves are solid and look great on the discs, the overall view of the sets physically is a bit cheap when compared to Arrow and they cost far, far too much for what we end up getting.

88FIlms

I would be remiss if i didn't mention The good lads over at 88 films who put out 36 Shaw's titles, really kickstarting this current wave of Shaw Brothers movies coming onto Bluray that we're seeing in the UK and US now. I really hope they continue to release more as some of their individual releases have been the absolute best out there in terms of presentation of the movie and some really well curated extras…You can check out a video that covers all 36 titles over on my Youtube channel, but for now i'll just pick a select few from their catalogue..

Eight Diagram Pole Fighter
Region B (UK)

Arguably Lau Kar Leung's best movie, and this release from 88 is fantastic (though Arrow Video's US release of the film tops it in terms of bonus features). The 88 FIlm's release features - Custom artwork from Kung Fu Bob O'Brien with a Poster, Audio Commentary from Scott Harrison and dual language Chinese and English Dubs.

Legendary Weapons of China
Region A(US)
Region B(UK)

Maybe 88's best single release to date in terms of bonus content, there are THREE audio commentaries, One by our own beloved Big Mike Leeder joined by fellow HK resident Arne Venema, a second track by other frequent Eastern Heroes contributors Frank Djeng & Michael Worth as well as a third track by Frank Djeng on his own. There are also archival interviews from Frederic Ambroisine's archives with Gordon Liu and Shaw's Producer Titus Ho, the original trailer for the movie as well as glorious custom Artwork once again by the insanely talented Kung Fu Bob (we also get a poster)

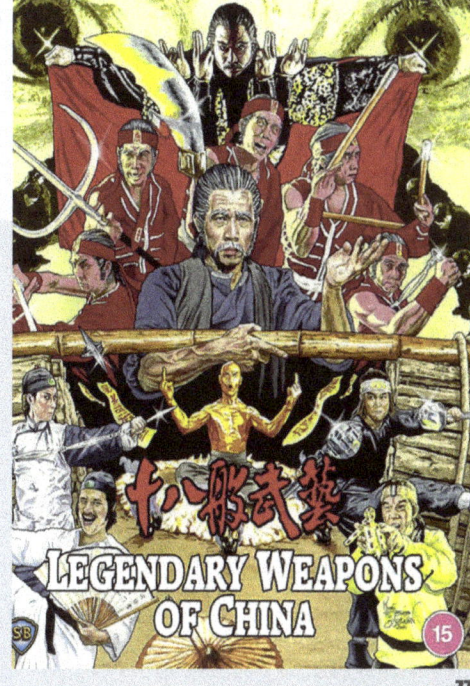

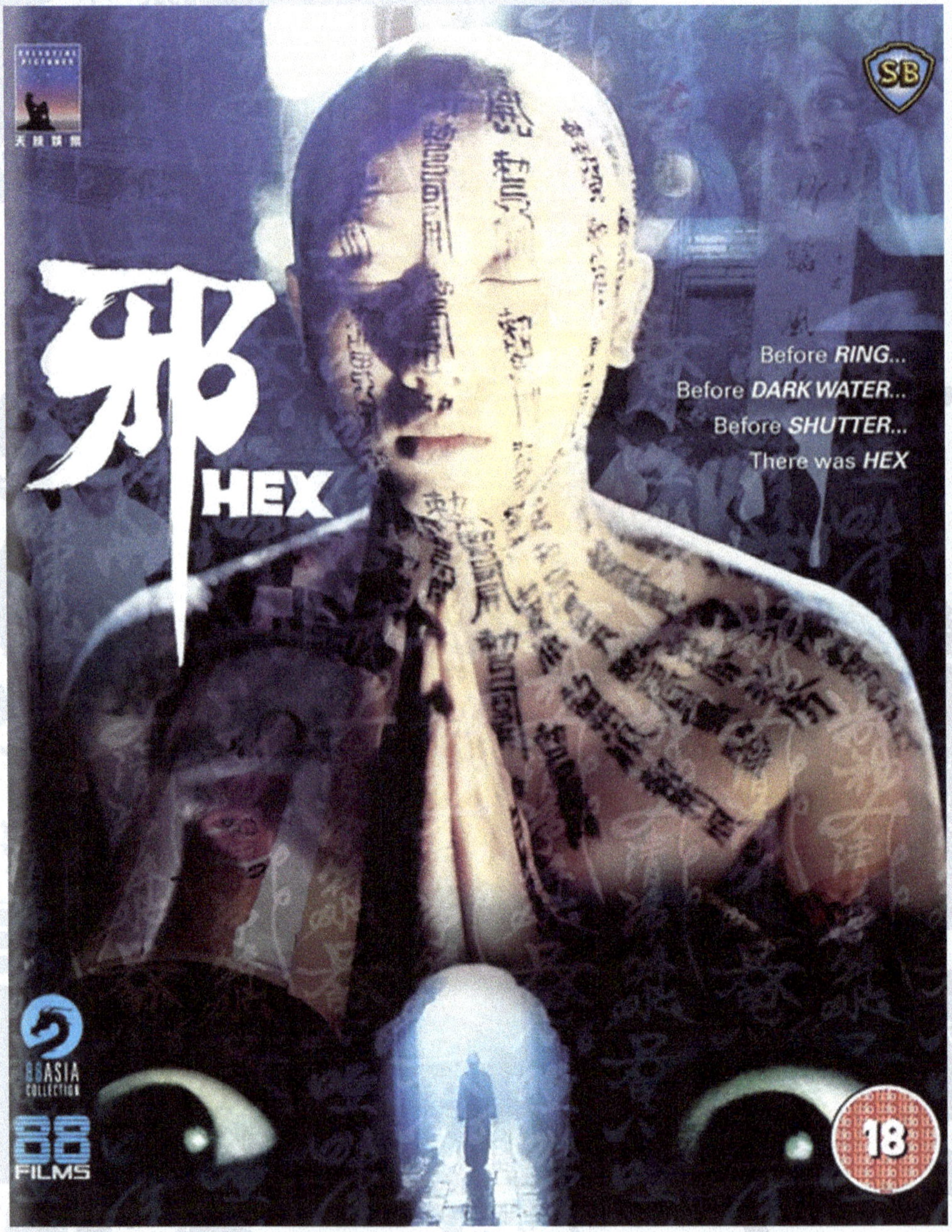

The One Armed Swordsman
Region B (UK)

This one is out of print now and can prove quite hard to get, but 88's release of the Jimmy Wang You classic the One Armed Swordsman remains the best version of the movie on Bluray thus far, The restoration looks incredible, there is also an interview with David West and an audio commentary from Bey Logan (from way, way back when he was still working with the label).

Martial Club
Region A (US)
Region B (UK)

Lau Kar Leung's other Wong Fei Hung movie, and the film with THAT incredible alleyway fight between Gordon Liu and Johnny Wang Lung Wei down an ever narrowing walled corridor - this release was one of 88's first to appear in both the UK AND the USA, comes with two commentary tracks, one by Frank DJeng flying solo and another where he is joined once more by Michael Worth as well as more excellent Frederic Ambroisine archival interviews, this time with Shaw's Villain Johnny Wang Lung Wei as well as with actor Robert Mak, Producer Lawrence Wong and another with stuntmen Hung Sun-Nam and Tony Tam. A loaded set, Kung fu Bob once more provided Cover Art duties.

Hex
Region B (UK)

This was 88's very first foray into Shaw's titles, it's spine #1 in their series, the wonderful HK reimagining of the old French thriller Diabolique, an a great slice of Psychological horror. Long out of print now, but highly recommended to try and track down!

The Vengeance Pack

Another smaller European label, TVP out of Germany have actually been putting out Shaw's movies for longer than almost any other label, they do stunning work in terms of restorations and sourcing deleted elements from the titles they release, some of them have English Subs, some do not, and they can be tricky to track down, but they've released the best versions thus far of some very notable titles…
Return of the One Armed Swordsman
The New One Armed Swordsman

Both titles came with English subs and both feature cover art by Kung Fu Bob. New One Armed Swordsman also has an audio commentary (in English) by Big Mike Leader and Arne Venema

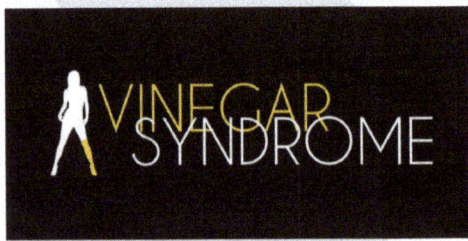

Vinegar Syndrome

File Vinegar Syndrome under, what is yet to come, as they've not actually put out any Shaw's titles so far, but are planning to this year…The American label have been turning their attention to more and more HK cinema over the past few years with excellent releases of some real HK classics, Righting Wrongs, Magic Crystal, The Iceman Cometh, Ebola Syndrome, Undeclared War, Burning Paradise and the Untold Story 2 to name a few…In October 2024 they'll be releasing Corpse Mania (1981) in 4K no less.

Spectrum Films

Spectrum Films in France have been quietly putting out a steady stream of Shaw's movies over the past three years, they tend to be overlooked by most of the western media due to them being specifically created for France only and as such having no English subtitles, but I like to keep an eye on what they're putting out and I've covered a fair few of their releases in previous issues of Eastern Heroes They're just about to release a triple pack of movies starring Tang Chia, Shaolin Prince, Shaolin Intruders and Opium and The Kung Fu Master as well as a Six Film Lau Kar Leung set, who brings together Legendary Weapons of China, Heroes of the East, Dirty Ho, Eight Diagram Pole Fighter, Martial Club as well as Cat Vs Rat, the set is notable as thus far nobody else anywhere in the world has put out Cat vs Rat onto Bluray…Another triple set in the works brings together Portrait in Crystal (another first onto Bluray anywhere in the world) Legend of the Fox and The Bells

of Death. Already in Spectrum's catalogue are two great double packs, one housing Holy Flame of the Martial World alongside the utterly insane Demon of The Lute, they also put out my own personal favourite of all their releases to date, a pack which brings together the two absolutely fantastic Bastard Swordsman movies. Doubles also exist for Gang Master & What Price Honesty, Secret Service of the Imperial Court & The Lady Assassin as well as two non Martial Arts features, both directed by Johnnie To Loving You & Lifeline - the firefighting drama. As previously mentioned, none of Spectrum's releases include English Subs or Audio Dubs, but for those that can speak Cantonese (or French) they're absolutely stunning releases, often with very well considered bonus features. That's your lot for just now dear friends, thanks for joining me in this dive into the various Boutique Labels and their hard work in bringing more and more Shaw Brothers classics onto the Bluray format over the past few years! Here's hoping we see more and more obscure titles from the Shaw's back catalogue seeing the light of day over the next few years. Whilst it seems like we've had a huge number of titles when looked at in a list like this, really we've barely scratched the surface of the studio's incredible back catalogue (they made close to 1000 movies during their prime between the 1960's - 1980's) Please follow me over on Youtube for more film reviews, Bluray Unboxings and lots, lots more Shaw Brothers content!

www.youtube.com/thefanaticaldragon

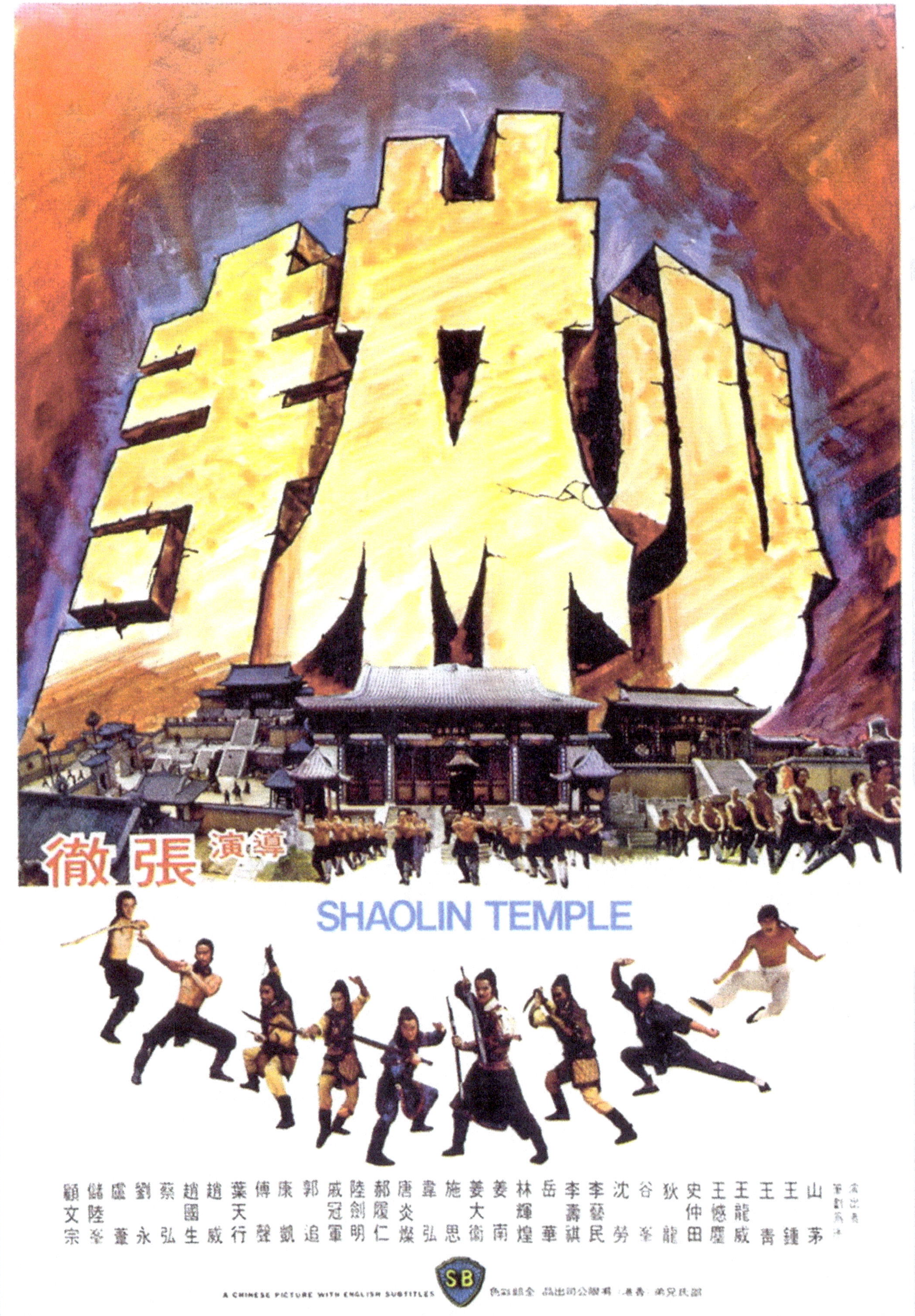
少林寺
導演 張徹
SHAOLIN TEMPLE
山茅
王鍾
王靑
王龍威
王憾塵
史仲田
狄龍
谷峯
沈勞
李藝民
李壽祺
岳華
林輝煌
姜南
姜大衛
施思
韋弘
唐炎燦
郝履仁
陸劍明
戚冠軍
郭追
康凱
傅聲
葉天行
趙威
趙國生
蔡弘
劉永
盧蕫
儲陸峯
顧文宗
SB
A CHINESE PICTURE WITH ENGLISH SUBTITLES

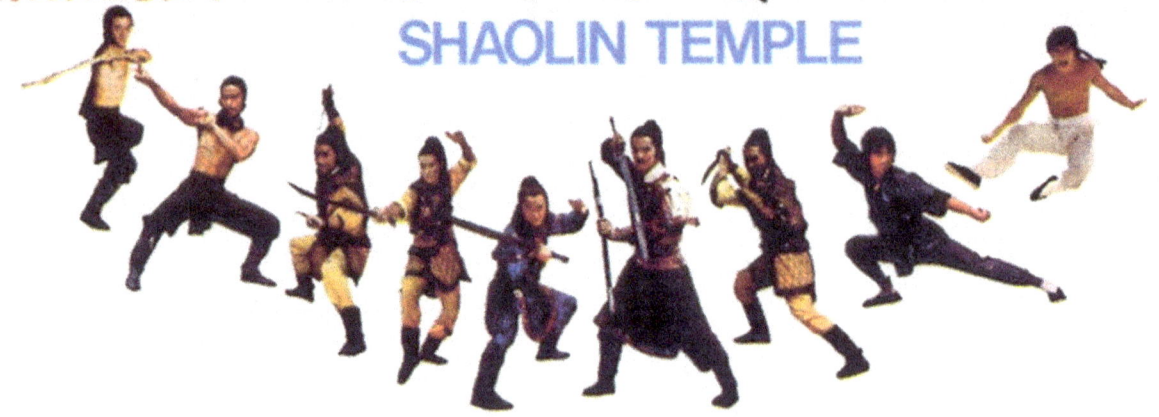

www.ingramcontent.com/pod-product-compliance
Lightning Source LLC
Chambersburg PA
CBHW042034100526
44587CB00029B/4419